KELVIN BURKE

LAKE OF TEARS

Does God weep in the face of suffering?

First published 2024

ISBN 978-1-9997082-5-2

Author: Kelvin Burke
© 2024 Springmead Publishing

All rights reserved. No part of this publication may be reproduced stored in or introduced into a retrieval system, or transmitted, in any form, or by any means (electronic, mechanical, photocopying, recording or otherwise) without the prior written permission of the publisher. Any person who does any unauthorised act in relation to this publication may be liable to criminal prosecution and civil claims for damages.

For licensing requests, please contact the publisher at
admin@springmead.org

Printed and bound in Poland.

This book is sold subject to the condition that is shall not, by way of trade or otherwise, be lent, re-sold, hired out, or otherwise circulated without the publisher's prior consent in any form of binding or cover other than that in which it is published and without a similar condition including this condition being imposed on the subsequent purchaser.

This book is memoir. It reflects the author's present recollections of experiences over time. Some names and characteristics have been changed, some events have been compressed, and some dialogue has been recreated. The rights of any business, product or place referred to either directly or indirectly in this work of fiction are hereby acknowledged.

Although the author and publisher have made every effort to ensure that the information in this book was correct at time of press, the author and publisher do not assume and hereby disclaim any liability to any party for any loss, damage, or disruption caused by errors or omissions, whether such errors or omissions result from negligence, accident, or any other cause.

Scriptures taken from the Holy Bible, New International Version®, NIV®. Copyright © 1973, 1978, 1984, 2011 by Biblica, Inc.™ Used by permission of Zondervan. All rights reserved worldwide. www.zondervan.com The 'NIV' and 'New International Version' are trademarks registered in the United States Patent and Trademark Office by Biblica, Inc.™

Scripture quotations marked (NLT) are taken from the Holy Bible, New Living Translation, copyright ©1996, 2004, 2015 by Tyndale House Foundation. Used by permission of Tyndale House Publishers, Carol Stream, Illinois 60188. All rights reserved.

Scripture quotations marked (NKJV) are taken from the New King James Version®. Copyright © 1982 by Thomas Nelson. Used by permission. All rights reserved.

www.kelvinburke.org
kelvin@kelvinburke.org

ACKNOWLEDGEMENTS

I am grateful to those who allowed me to share their stories as they interlocked with my own journey of faith. Several people read the manuscript and helped me improve it. Chloé Bell, Jennie Burke, Ali Hull, Chris Kane, and Jacqueline Smith Nelson, to name a few. Others have supported me through the maze of publishing. Sincerest thanks to you: Pete Greig, Simon Ponsonby, Sharon and Robert Hastings, Peter Spreckley, Marcus Thomas, Gwen Mills, Barrie Lawrence, Steve Gravett and Hanspeter Nuesch.

I am indebted to the Accountancy world that let me in and the clients who trusted me with their business and financial affairs. To Cranmer, the bible college that honed me and the churches, St Peter's and St Andrew's, who gave me a start.

I cannot thank enough, the NHS, who were not shackled by my disability or diversity. A special thanks to Christ Swift and Tony Ruddle, who showed me, by example, the difference that healthcare Chaplains can make in delivering holistic care to all.

I am especially grateful to Chloé Rosetta Bell, who managed the typesetting, editing, and publishing process – a real labour of love. Your reward is in heaven.

Finally, thank you to Gracelyn and Layla-Thea for being a recent part of my life. Thank you for springing off your parents, Katie and Dylan and Chloé and Dan, plus Ellie and Ben, my lovely family who have supported me throughout the toil of writing.

Last but not least, to Jennie, my primus inter pares, this is our story, and I am so grateful for your friendship, love and patience in the ten years that I have been harping on about this. You truly are my soul mate.

CONTENTS

INTRODUCTION		7
CHAPTER 1	BEGINNINGS	11
CHAPTER 2	SAVED	19
CHAPTER 3	TROUBLES	29
CHAPTER 4	MOVING ON	37
CHAPTER 5	STARTING OUT	49
CHAPTER 6	HONISTER	57
CHAPTER 7	LEARNING TO WALK AGAIN	69
CHAPTER 8	LEARNING TO LIVE AGAIN	83
CHAPTER 9	LAKE OF TEARS	103
CHAPTER 10	BUSINESS MATTERS	123
CHAPTER 11	GUIDED	137
CHAPTER 12	CALLED	147
CHAPTER 13	HOMECOMING	159
CHAPTER 14	CHAPLAIN	173
CHAPTER 15	RITA	189
CHAPTER 16	ALL THIS BEAUTY	195
EPILOGUE	LAKE OF TEARS: REVISITED	213
GLOSSARY		219

Introduction

I resist the temptation to call this book a memoir. That would serve only to be a tracker of my own life. I prefer to settle for that old-fashioned word, 'testimony'. This is my testimony of what God does in and through lives where He has been given Lordship. I shall not give a spoiler in this introduction, suffice to say, an encounter with God when I was at a low ebb with a barrage of questions broke through my tough exterior. Those queries that seemed unanswered and possibly unheard were personally replied to when the divine mysteriously spoke to me. It has taken years of reflection to realise how important that encounter was.

This is an ordinary story of a young boy brought up in a Christian home in peacetime Northern Ireland. The beautiful Armagh countryside was like a large playground to adventurers such as I. That peace was shattered by the period in Ireland's history now referred to as the 'Troubles.' Urban dwellers had far more experience of the reality of what that meant, but, for us rural types, there were plenty of tales of paramilitary brutality and subterfuge that wrought terror to our picturesque province. The impact on me, you could say, was minimal, but it did shape my thinking and my wanderings. Crossing the

Irish Sea to study at Manchester University, I revelled in the cauldron of sport, academia, and faith. It set me up very well for a move to West Yorkshire, where I worked in accountancy, youth work and then ordained ministry – first as a Reverend in Church and later as a Reverend in Healthcare Chaplaincy.

A defining moment and a life-changing road traffic accident (RTA) took me on a different trajectory from what I had imagined life might hold. This book testifies that God is an ever-present help in those times of trouble. True, I lost a lot on that fateful day in England's beautiful Lake District – unfulfilled sporting dreams and work opportunities, not to mention the physicality of paralysis. On the other hand, I gained a hope in God that has buoyed me and sustained me throughout the years that followed. Of course, that hope is rooted in a decision I made as a young Ulster lad to place my trust and confidence in the Lord Jesus Christ. That was, by far, the greatest personal transformation that occurred in my lifetime. For the nearly sixty years that have ensued, Christ has been with me always, never left me and, never let me down. If you do not have faith, you will find that hard to believe, but that is what this testimony is about.

I said my accident was a defining moment in my life, but I have refused to let it define me. What does define me, what makes me tick, is the everyday personal relationship I have with my Lord and Saviour. I wish there was a jargon-free way of saying that, but that is my lived experience, my daily reality. I hope you can cut me some slack and read on.

My life in the world of business and finance was hunky-dory and something I was groomed and destined for since my school days. I could even witness God at work in mysterious ways through the vocation of Chartered Accountancy. I managed to refer to a few situations where that was true in Chapter Ten. Consequently, it took an encounter with a geranium plant to wrench me away from that genre.

Moving to the beautiful historic city of Durham to study Theology with a young family in tow was a special privilege and a real joy. Our third girl was born during that time and some of my time set aside in pursuit of training took place on beaches and play areas. Nonetheless, it was a genuine time of ministerial formation. Cranmer and the Arts Centre church plant were very significant to the young Burke family. I tried to capture the drama of my time in the North East in Chapter Twelve.

Just as I was surprised by joy in Durham, I was then surprised to be back in Yorkshire as a Reverend, and it was not too long before I morphed into a hospital chaplain on the payroll of the NHS. The accident that introduced me to the world of chaplains who tended my spirituality subliminally drew me into active service in that world. It has been a ministry that enlivened me, and the daily encounters with those of faith and those of no faith gave me fresh insights into my 'Lake of Tears' musings. I trust that in sharing these with you in the closing chapters you will (in the words of Ephesians 5:19) 'grasp how wide and long and high and deep is the love of God', not only for those in healthcare but also for you.

Thank you for reading this far. Now, on with the rest!

I pray that you will be blessed.

Kelvin

ONE

Beginnings

I was saturated in the beck, pinned beneath the Morris. There was an eerie silence. Six men lifted the car off my crushed torso, a voice bellowed, 'Crawl out!'

I was barely conscious but so aware that I was trapped under the vehicle and immersed in the river, unable to help myself and incapable of drawing my next breath.

As commanded, I tried to gather my legs under me to crawl to the safety of the steep embankment. I was fit and strong and sporty; surely, I could muster the strength to save myself as the car lifters held the 1960s Morris Traveller several feet aloft.

To my horror, the mental instruction from brain to limbs was not obeyed. Somehow, in my watery confusion, I understood that my legs would not function and my injuries were serious. I had no alternative but to submit to the elements and abandon fruitless efforts to scramble to the water's edge. Helpless, sodden and cold, a hazy darkness came over me. I lay crumpled like a car-struck dog waiting for the death knell.

A couple of good Samaritans took hold of my navy hoody, emblazoned 32 in bright orange, and dragged me, hood and shoulder, to the inhospitable grassy scrub.

My eyes looked towards the steep, rugged escarpment of Honister Crag on Fleetwith Pike. Climbers, like precarious matchstick men, looked down on me. Some had already run to my aid and were part of my human carjack. A passing doctor parked and scurried down the incline to oversee the tending. The medic denied enthusiastic men-of-braun's request to firemans-lift me to the roadside. That would surely have ended the feeble life I had. Instead, we waited until the distant 'nee-naw' of the ambulance came to my rescue in answer to the 999 call.

The GP's hunch was a spinal injury. As paramedics strapped me tightly into a fibreglass stretcher that matched the colour of my 32, the doctor slipped away; his job was done, and a life had been saved. Providentially, we met again a year later at a businessmen's breakfast in Bradford. I was overjoyed to shake the hand of the man who oversaw my care on that ghastly bank of Honister. He was a Godsend, a life preserver.

We were just two miles from the safety of our campsite base at Grange in Borrowdale, but it seemed a million miles away as I faded in and out of consciousness. My mind drifted back to safer times and the ash-blonde, pint-sized young rascal who loved to climb trees. The daredevil child who enjoyed terrifying his parents, jumping, climbing and calling out from Cornascriebe treetops. The peaceful years of growing up in Northern Ireland's Armagh countryside and colloquial banter with Ulster farmers were blurrily entwined with panic commands of Honister friends calling, 'Hold on,' 'You will be all right' and 'Hang in there, Kel' as they winched the stretcher to the roadside.

The road from there to Whitehaven was a vale of shakes and aches. I sucked hard on oxygen while the paramedic reassuringly, at ten-minute intervals, said that we were ten minutes from our destination. Ninety minutes later, I was admitted to the Intensive Care Unit of West Cumberland Hospital.

I still had the capacity to inform the admissions clerk that I was born in 1956 in Portadown, Northern Ireland. As I drifted into an induced slumber, I wondered who would alert Billy and Rita Burke. In three days' time, I was due to meet up with Mum and Dad at a Conference in Blackpool. There would be no meeting; I was tethered to a hospital bed with lines and tubes, masks and drips. Once again, I was helpless, unable to reach my loved ones.

I was the middle of three brothers: Harry, four years older, and Richard, eight years younger. We were nurtured in the Christian way. There were great expectations that Billy's three boys would perpetuate the family business, a firm that was built on Christian values of honesty, hard work, and total commitment. 'Burkes of Cornascriebe' was well known in Ulster as one of the main tractor and farm machinery dealerships and general merchants. The business was first established in 1911, and Billy continued in the footsteps of my grandfather William Henry Burke, supplying anything from grain to groceries to the farming community in the orchard County of Armagh, 'the apple of Ireland's green eye.'

Billy Burke did not suffer fools, especially imprudent employees who could endanger the company's Christian integrity. If 'the boss' told you off, you knew about it! Nonetheless, 'Billy' was well-loved, and his loyalty and affection for staff and customers was truly reciprocal.

The 'firm hand' was also part of our childhood, and 'wait till your dad gets home' was a motherly threat us boys didn't like to hear. We were taught sound Christian principles; to honour the Sabbath, respect our elders, put others first and to 'love the Lord with all your heart.' These were our 'family values,' with obvious echoes of the Ten Commandments. It was also instilled in our upbringing that we were not born Christians just because our parents were believers; you 'must be born again.' Dad often said, 'One day, you'll have to make your own mind up whether you will walk with the Lord or walk away from him.' It's a message I took on board and one I have passed on to many others throughout my own life.

My father was a founding member of the Full Gospel Businessmen's Fellowship International in Ireland (FGBMFI). Commissioned personally by Demos Shakarian: Hector Crory, Harry Ferguson, and Billy Burke spearheaded the Belfast Chapter of the FGBMFI.

As a youth, I loved to listen to the stories of how God was active throughout the world, shaping Christian businesses and farms and transforming the lives of these 'Happiest People on Earth,' as FGB Founder Shakarian put it. From a young age, I longed to see God's dynamic Holy Spirit at work in my own life.

Despite being a leader in business, Billy Burke was a quiet man, working backstage rather than being in the spotlight.

Mum was the opposite. As a result of a miraculous healing from a near-fatal horse-riding accident, my mother, Rita Burke, became well-known as a public speaker, telling her story and calling people to 'lean on the promises' of God. Specifically, she had a public ministry of laying on hands and 'praying for the sick.'

'I am not a faith healer,' I often heard her explain on the telephone, 'it is divine healing, I pray, and God through Jesus is the healer.'

Rita travelled widely in the USA, Canada and Europe to speak at conferences and 'to minister to the sick.'

We were unimpressed, on her return from these trips, to hear about her TV and radio interviews, preferring as youngsters to ask, 'What did you bring us home?'

Our home in Cornascriebe was a constant flow of needy people who made appointments to receive prayer from Rita Burke.

It was 'normal' in my childhood to witness miracles of healing and the Holy Spirit showering 'blessings' on grateful visitors to our home. In all my years, I have never seen anyone with the boldness my mother had in prayer for the 'healing of the sick.' I recall one instance in Portadown when Mum was clothes shopping with me in tow. The shop assistant said, in passing, that she was feeling ill, and Mum asked her to take a seat in the fitting booth. With the curtains pulled, she 'laid on hands' and prayed for healing! Us three boys learnt to keep quiet about headaches and queasy tummies; otherwise, mum would clamp those hands on, and we would have to sit sometimes for 30 or 45 minutes while the ailment was 'prayed over.'

Rita was the sixth child of Minnie and Willy-John (Granda) McMurray of Ballynagarrick. Granda was a beef and poultry farmer, a tall, rugged man with a great head of hair and family charisma in no small measure. He was a long-distance runner and a Gospel preacher in the local churches. He used to boast to me that he would drink six raw eggs before each race. It was a beverage he demonstrated to me several times. In those days, salmonella was the name of a female fish!

My daredevil traits were finely honed on Granda McMurray's farm; climbing loosely packed hay bales and swinging like a chimpanzee from rafters, sprinting through 'the-field-where-the-bull-was,' and bashing rats trapped in meal bins before they could run up the leg of my trousers!

Granda taught me a practical lesson on humility that became a personal rule of life:

'Let's go and feed the chickens, and I'll show ye something,' he said as he led me outside his scullery and into the cobbled farmyard in the shadow of the cluster of outbuildings. As he picked up a well-bashed metal bucket and half filled it with 'hen-meal,' he said, 'Watch this.'

Granda began making clucking noises and calling, 'Here, Chucky, Chucky.'

About a dozen brown hens emerged from nowhere.

He 'sowed' the meal across the dirt in the farmyard, and the hens shuffled and shoved, fought and squawked in their efforts to get in pole position for their afternoon treat. It wasn't long before the kafuffle quietened, and the bolder hens pecked their fill as the less gregarious sisters loitered in the background.

'That's the way of the world,' Granda McMurray explained, 'they have worked out a 'pecking order.' From the most dominant right down to the last one, a clear pecking order was established.

Granda added, 'Kelvin, wherever you go and whatever you do, you will see people working out a pecking order. When you stand around 'small-talking' after a funeral or a business meeting, you'll hear them asking about sales, about produce, how many people work for you, and what type of car you drive. They're working out a pecking order until some big shot is the top hen, and someone who can't afford a suit and cuff links is at the bottom of the pile.' I understood what he meant as he delivered the lesson;

'Kelvin, our Lord was the only one worthy in the history of this world to be the top hen, but he turned that whole thing on its head by saying we must become like servants to others (Mark 10 :44). He said, 'The first must be last,' and in John's gospel, he took a towel and a bowl of water and went around his 12 disciples and washed their feet (John Chapter 13).'

Granda put his hand on my head and ruffled my blonde hair before resting his reassuring arm on my shoulder as we walked back to the scullery; 'Kelvin, when you get older, remember to take the low place. Humble people give the glory to God.' He continued, 'The Lord Jesus was in his heavenly place, but he humbled himself to become one of us, a human being, he took the low place for you, Kelvin' (Philippians 2:3). Turning to Granny he said, 'Put the kettle on Minnie, we're going to make a preacher out of this one!'

I loved Granda McMurray dearly, and he took special notice of my interest in his itinerant evangelist's tales. His lessons continued to instruct me long after he had gone to be with the Lord.

Laid naked in the Intensive Care Unit at West Cumberland Hospital, my denim jeans and 32-emblazoned sweatshirt cut from my frame, I began to regain consciousness. The tiny bible I had read six hours earlier was recovered from my back pocket, wet and walloped, a testament of survival. I wondered if I was going to survive or if would I go to be with Granda and Jesus. The past mingled with the present in that fragile place, and I prayed a desperate prayer, 'Lord, don't take me now; I have so much to live for, so much that I want to do for you.'

TWO

Saved!

'I think your son must be accident prone', nurse Luton joked with mother. 'No, he just likes climbing, football, cricket, and generally glyping and gallivanting around,' mum replied.

It was my fifth admission to Lurgan Hospital in two years, and I had not yet reached my eleventh birthday. Five broken arms in two years left Mum wondering how she would usher me safely through adolescence. I loved sport, and I loved climbing, and the more fear I saw in other people's faces, the more daring I became.

My first broken arm came about from playing football. My second happened when I fell from an apple tree. The branch I stood on broke, and I tumbled. For the third break, I fell from our attic onto the landing. The door was closed, not fastened, I stepped on it, and it sprung open like a gallows trap door. The fourth was a cracked wrist from falling from a tractor and another spell in Lurgan Hospital Children's ward. I was on personal terms with the nursing staff; on several occasions, I proposed to Nurse Luton, vowing that I would marry her if she could wait for me to grow up! My childhood crush on the matron was not the reason I dared to climb and fall a fifth time!

That last 'fall' was almost my last testament. Sullivan's birthday party was a great party to be invited to. They had a farm with loads of outhouses for 'cowboys and injuns' to role-play. I was the foolhardy rancher who climbed up the bales of hay in Sullivan's hayshed. The pyramid-like route to the roof-rafters was an invitation I couldn't resist. Perched at the haystack summit, this cowboy hung over the rafter and took aim at an 'injun' below. The savage fired back, and I jumped from the stanchion onto the top hay bales. Unfortunately, my momentum dislodged the bale, and I tumbled to the ground and lay motionless on the concrete below. I was rushed to Lurgan Hospital, concussed with suspected head injuries and more broken bones. Mum was waiting for me at A&E, and nurse Luton on the children's ward was on hand to admit me for the fifth time.

The end result was a dislocated left shoulder and broken arm above the elbow. The head survived! It was another plaster cast and a spell in Lurgan Hospital. This time, I felt I had been fortunate, and even at this young age, I realised how fragile life can be.

Away from school, I spent most of my time outdoors. Playing football, climbing or catching sticklebacks in a jam jar in the crystal-clear streams of the irrigation 'shucks' around my dad's fields. There wasn't a lot to do indoors, I didn't read much, and I kept the stamp and coin collecting for rainy days. Mum paid me a 'tanner' if I read a chapter of my bible and a shilling if I could memorise key verses. This bribery gave me my early grounding in the scriptures; it stood me in good stead.

There was no Television in our home in the 1960s. While my

friends chatted at school break times about 'last night's telly,' I was ashamed to admit that we weren't allowed to own one. My father said TV was 'worldly' and it would 'lead us away from the Lord.' In the 1960s, TV was big news, and well-off people even had a 'colour telly.'

Despite television being 'worldly,' Granda McMurray had one. It seemed that news and nature programmes were not as 'worldly' as some of the other 'rubbish' that was on. Sport was another grey area when it came to 'worldliness,' I was allowed to visit Granda's to see the football, and if I didn't tell Mum, he'd let me watch the boxing or the wrestling!

Perhaps it was because I had no television and no appetite for reading that the outdoors became my playground. I would double dare myself to step stone across streams, jump ditches and then settle down to build dams to catch the wee fish whilst chewing a penny bubbly until I had cramp in my jaws. Me and my friend Paul rode our bikes with cardboard in the spokes to make them sound like motorbikes. Riding at top speed down Glenoran Hill hanging the hoods of our coats on our heads with the rest of the garment flying in the slipstream. That was better than staying in and reading 'Look and Learn' or 'Tiger and Hurricane.'

My brother Harry and I would spend hours building go-carts out of old pallets and wheels from scraps of old prams and trolleys. We would walk to the top of 'Blacks Hill' and set off at top speed down the slope, only to remember that we had no brakes! After running into ditches to avoid oncoming vehicles a few times, we learned to solve the problem, to break with the soles of our feet on the front wheels. Our early years were a catalogue of cuts, purple bruises and broken bones and teeth. We learned two things in the rough and tumble of growing up at Cornascriebe: we learned to get over it, and we learned not to do the same thing again! Health and Safety was not invented in our townland in the 1960s! Ironically, Harry ended up in Rally Cross racing while I ended up with a different type of wheels.

I learned to drive a tractor before I left Primary School. There was no instructor, just a key in the ignition, a Fordson Major in the farmyard and my dad's fields to aim for. I recall standing with both feet on the tractor's brakes as the beast careered into a dunghill. No one told me about clutching; I just learned the hard way!

I have fond memories of bringing the hay in, the golden fields, the men at work, the dust rising towards the summer sun. As a youngster, I didn't feel the rush and panic of getting it all cut, shaken, baled and brought in while the sun shone. I just liked the sense of everybody pulling together to get the job done.

Sam Courtney was Burke's workshop foreman, but all of the men 'mucked in' in the fields when it was harvest time.

Sam used to call me 'Teddy' because of an all-in-one suit I wore when I was learning to walk. He took a special interest in my development as a fledgling tractor driver. One day, I managed to talk Sam into letting me have a go at ploughing. He sat me down on the mudguard and told me to watch him plough. I spent my lesson looking ahead and looking back at the lovely straight furrows he turned over.

When it came to my turn, Sam sat on the wheel guard, and I could hear him shouting, 'Easy-on, Teddy, Easy-on,' as I opened the throttle and steered all over the place. The wheel was jerking this way and that, and I looked back and saw broken furrows and dogs' hind-leg tracks. I remember thinking that I had wrecked the whole field. Sam reassured me, 'Don't worry about it, Teddy; it'll all grow corn in the end.'

I took a special interest in that field that year. I knew roughly what was Sam's bit, and what was my mess. True enough, as Sam had predicted, the seed was sown, and the corn took well. By the summer, my heart leapt to see one golden field of corn, not two broken Courtney and Burke sections. It was as if, in time, the mistakes and wrong turns I had taken had been redeemed by the work of the sun and rain on the seed. Later in life, I came to appreciate those golden fields as a metaphor for the Lord whispering to me that I could have a fresh start no matter what mess I made by returning to God in prayer. I often think that I don't deserve the golden cornfield of blessings that God brings about. It is a good picture of God's grace and mercy.

In the summer of '66, I heard about a 'tent mission' in Ahorey, and Sam Workman was 'preaching the Gospel' every evening for a week. The marquee was packed each sunny summer's evening. The side flaps were lifted so that latecomers could stand and hear 'the message' from outside. By Saturday, the sawdust on the grass had compacted into the hard field base, and Pastor Workman stood on the makeshift wooden pulpit to 'deliver the word.' The ladies in the choir in their white mohair berets had sung 'the anthem' and sat listening attentively to the Pastor. Dad brought me to the meetings, and I remember looking around at the people from our townland, farmers and their families, boys from Ahorey Sunday School, workers from 'Ulster Meats' and some of Burkes' staff as well. The 'boss' must have told them they needed to attend, and if the boss told you, you attended.

I remember more about the preacher's tone of voice than I do about the message. That is, except for the Saturday night. The preacher introduced Saturday's message as the last chance in this mission to make peace with God.

He took Matthew 24:36 for his theme and stated, 'no one knows the hour or the day…of Jesus Christ's return.'

'Friends,' Pastor Workman spoke softly, 'if you leave here tonight without knowing Jesus as your personal Saviour, you are gambling with time and eternity. You don't know when your hour may come to see Jesus face to face.'

Something spoke deep into my heart that I did not know Jesus in that personal way. I knew about Jesus; I had seen him at work through my parents and in the lives of Bob Downey and Sunday School teachers like Edmund Greer and Tommy Foster, but I didn't know Jesus personally. I hadn't done what the Pastor was talking about; I'd never invited him into my life, and Rev Workman said Jesus would not push himself into your life; he 'stands at the door knocking' and you have to invite him in. My heart started to beat a little faster. I sensed that the preacher was talking to me alone. In the midst of hundreds in that tent mission, it was as if I was the only one there.

The preacher increased his oratory volume and read Matthew 24:40, 'Then two men will be working in the field, one will be taken and one left…' My thoughts jumped to Sam Courtney ploughing in the field with me on the mudguard of the wheel, 'one would be taken and one left.' In my youthful understanding of the evangelist's message, I thought that I would be one of the ones who would be left. Despite all my religious upbringing, my dad's words echoed in my mind; 'you can't be born Christian; you must be born again.' These words of Jesus from John 3:7 came back to me as I sat challenged by Pastor Workman. 'Marvel not that I said unto thee, Ye must be born again.'

His conclusion seemed to be a barrage of questions, all of

them spoken directly to me; 'Will you take that step tonight?' 'Are you ready to make peace with God?' 'Are you sure your name is written in the Book of Life?' 'If you were to die tonight, where would your soul go - to eternity with Christ or a Christ-less eternity?' 'Can you sense that Jesus is standing at the door of your life, knocking and waiting to be invited in?' 'Will you make that important step tonight?'

The preacher lowered his tone to dulcet and continued, 'Now I am going to ask each and every one of you to bow your heads and close your eyes as we pray.' He reassuringly repeated the crowd's posture; 'as every eye is closed and every head is bowed, I want you to put your hand up to say, 'I want to invite Jesus into my life.' Sam Workman paused and interjected the waiting with, 'God bless you, I see that hand', and to another who must have been waving excessively, he said, 'You can put your hand down now, brother; the Lord knows your decision.' I could see through the partially opened fingers in my 'praying hands' that some other people were peeping too. Hands were raised and lowered all over the place, but not every eye was closed! This proved to be a deterrent to my own responding.

The Pastor waited a while longer; this was my night; I knew what I needed to do; I could feel the tension, the pressure to 'just slip your hand up as a sign of saying yes to Jesus.' Pastor Workman said, 'I know there is someone else here tonight who wants to respond.' It was me; I wanted to, I needed to, and I would be left in the field if Jesus came back. I could hear my heart beating in my chest, and I imagined the whole Ahorey mission tent could hear that pulse.

'I'll just wait a moment, longer, and then I'll pray, God bless you, sister…'

The 'moment longer' was not as long as I had expected.

Rev. Workman brought the curtain down on this evening's mission with a closing prayer. I had missed the opportunity! His concluding prayer for everyone who had responded was not for me. I had failed to respond in time; the nerves got the better of me, and I bottled it when I needed to be brave and put my hand up for the Lord. I felt such a failure as the ladies in their mohair bonnets sang, 'Amazing grace, how sweet the sound that saved a wretch like me.' Their anthem was like a knife piercing my soul; I was heartbroken, I was a wretch all right, but I wasn't saved! 'I once was lost, but now I'm found'…. I was still lost. The preacher gave a final blessing and thanked many people for helping with the week's mission. People stood up in a disorderly way and left the mission tent through the side flaps and into the fresh country air as the sun set in a peachy sky for the final night of the Ahorey mission.

I walked at a skipping pace to keep up with my father's large strides as we headed for our Woolsey 16/60. 'Come on, boy,' he said, 'let's get to the car first and beat the traffic.' I thought he should be able to sense my dilemma. I was not saved. If Jesus comes back tonight, I will be left, and my dad wants to 'beat the traffic.' The futility of his haste mocked the tragedy that had just occurred. I missed the altar call! My name was not in the 'Book of Life,' and if we crashed on the way home, I would not go to be with Jesus! And to add insult to injury, my dad didn't appreciate my predicament.

The 1760 yards to our home were uneventful; my father said I was quiet, and I stayed quiet. 'What did you think of Pastor Workman?' he enquired.

'He was good' was all I could offer.

In fact, Workman had condemned me to a 'Christless eternity', but like the bruises from all the go-cart crashes, I would have to get over it.

Dusk faded to dark, and I got ready for bed; my eternal damnation weighed heavy on my mind. Mum uttered the customary prayer and sent me to bed. I lay in bed, reliving my wasted opportunity at the Ahorey tent mission. I began to cry and sob, fearing that the Lord may come back that night and Mum and Dad would be taken, and I would be left. I imagined going into their bedroom the next morning and finding I was alone at home and living in a world with all the people who did not believe in Jesus as a personal saviour. The bedroom door opened, and my mother came in and sat on my bed. 'What's wrong with you, Kelvin?' she enquired.

I sobbed as I poured out my heart to her and let her into the secret that I wasn't saved, and I had missed my altercall.

I felt Mum's reassuring embrace and encouraging words, 'It's Okay, it's all going to be Okay,' she said. 'Sam Workman doesn't make you a Christian,' she said. 'The tent mission is only one way to become a Christian. You can become a Christian in the quietness of your own heart,' she explained. 'When Jesus said to Nicodemus, 'You must be born again,' Sam Workman wasn't there. Jesus simply meant that you need to ask him to give you a new start, a new life secure in Jesus. That's what being born again means.'

I asked my mother what I could do about it now, and she said she would leave the room and told me to get out of bed and get onto my knees and say out loud this prayer, 'Come into my heart, Lord Jesus, forgive me my past sins, thank you for dying on the cross for me. Now, I receive your new and eternal life.'

The door closed, and I leapt out of bed for fear of the curtain falling on this opportunity. As I knelt and prayed those words my mum had taught me, I felt a peace in my innermost parts, perhaps that's my soul, that I was saved! I would not perish because I now had eternal life. There were no flashes of lightning, no neon signs saying, 'Well done, my good and faithful one.' Becoming a Christian was unspectacular but nonetheless transformational.

THREE

Troubles

With childlike simplicity, I prayed that 'believer's prayer' when I was ten years old. My first experience of the dynamic of the Holy Spirit came when I was fourteen. One of the FGBMFI speakers who was staying in our 'visitors room' spoke with me about the second chapter of Acts and Pentecost. Under his guidance, I prayed for the Baptism in the Holy Spirit. It is difficult to describe the experience that followed; suffice to say, in the words of John Wesley, my heart was 'strangely warmed', and I was overcome with joy.

As I began to express my limited vocabulary of gratitude to God, the words became less significant and then, without forcing it, developed into a new prayer language. The evening was gone in a flash; I was exhausted in a glorious way, I felt drenched in a baptismal way, and I knew I would never be the same after this out-pouring. This gift has continued to be both a treasure and an empowering throughout my life.

Looking back, it was a strange decision, at the age of eleven, to leave home. In the autumn of 1967, I left Portadown and became a border at a Quaker school - Friends School Lisburn. Lisburn was just ten miles from Northern Ireland's capital. Belfast was a peaceful, busy, bustling business city, standing on the banks of the River Lagan, which flowed from Slieve Croobe through Lisburn to the mouth of Belfast Lough. How that peace was to be shaken over the years that ensued.

The decision to study at a Quaker school had more to do with an aunt's influence and Primary school companions than religious denominations or academia. Dad's sister, Auntie Joan, was a Quaker, and Cousin Dinah was a prefect there. They both gave 'Friends' a good write-up. The Piele's and Lamb's, synonymous with Fruitfield Jam, were sending their children there. Harry, Lawrence, David and Judith, in year 6, persuaded me that boarding at Friends would be a life-changing experience. It certainly was. In addition, mothers travelling with the Christian' healing ministry was a contributing factor to the grand decision. Thus, at the age of 11¼, I relocated to Ardfallen, the junior boy's dorms under Jack and Katie Shemeld's regime. There were shoe inspections before lights-out, behind-the-neck and ears inspections before uniform-on and detention for misdemeanours involved writing the preface of Quakerism, first published in 1672.

From the outset, I was desperately lonely and tried to persuade my parents that we had made a bad decision.

I pleaded with them to let me move back home to Portadown, but we decided to give it a term rather than make a rash decision. I cried myself to sleep many nights, wishing I were home with my family in Cornascriebe. I got great comfort from reading my bible and, in prayer, sharing my grief and burdens with my Lord Jesus. My new faith was surely put to the test in more ways than loneliness.

My fellow Borders thought it a novelty to have someone reading the bible before 'lights out.' In truth, there were several skirmishes in the dorms, and I confess that I retaliated in an un-Christ-like way. In time, my peers grew to respect my spiritual 'quiet times', and news travelled around the school that 'KB' was religious but that he was 'Okay.'

Being active in sport, drew me into the 'in crowd' but being 'good-living' put me on the periphery. The red lapel badge on my school blazer that said 'Jesus Saves' became the butt of many-a-jibe. 'Jesus saves….green shield stamps,' one would say, 'Jesus saves…..at Ulster Bank,' another quipped. 'Jesus saves, but George Best scores the rebound' was one of my favourites. It was cruel banter, but I could see the humour in it. Many times, older boys grabbed me by the lapels and roughed me up, ordering me to 'take the ***** badge off', but it became a part of my Christian witness, and refusing to remove it was my way of 'standing firm' for the Lord.

Some of the Christian teachers started a Christian Union, which met weekly at lunchtime and was a real encouragement to me to stay close to the Lord in quiet times of prayer and bible study. Miss Burgess was one of those who led by example. Her good looks, long blonde hair and constant bubbly personality made it 'all right' to be a Christian. In the classroom, she was a stern 'take no prisoners' maths teacher, but after lessons, she was a mentor and friend who would ask, 'How are things going with you and the Lord?' Teachers like Barbara Burgess looking out for us 'believers' were a real boost as we grew spiritually and physically. Long after their tuition was forgotten, their qualities of kindness and generosity and going the 'extra mile' endures.

Older pupils were another source of encouragement. My mentor was Brian Hanna, two years older than me, and a

Christian. He was a leading sportsman in the school, an all-rounder at Rugby, Hockey and Cricket and many times Brian helped me 'hang in there' with God and be a 'good witness.'

As a border at school, there was plenty of spare time for sport. I spent hours practising hockey skills after school with other borders who had nothing better to do. In my time at Friends School, I received my 'colours' for hockey and for table tennis. I was 'Capped' for Ulster Schoolboys' hockey X1 in my final year at school.

The Civil Rights movement and accusations of gerrymandering had passed me by at school and in Cornascriebe. Slowly, we began to hear about young people who had been 'tarred and feathered' because a Catholic girl was dating a soldier or a Protestant boy was courting a Catholic girl. The local papers carried stories about men who had been 'knee-capped' for fraternising with the British Army. News of torture and terrorism all over the province spread like wildfire. There was a change in the air, peace was threatened, and it became relevant whether you were a 'left or a right footer.'

Northern Ireland in the 1970s was a very different place from the years before. Most days, the train from Portadown to Lisburn was stoned and hailed with ball bearings projected by homemade catapults. Bomb hoaxes were commonplace on our train and at school.

Lisburn was just ten miles south of Belfast and came under terrorist attacks on several occasions. Besides that, we could hear the dull thud of the Belfast explosions carried along the Lagan Valley. As schoolboys, we would engage in banal conversations in the aftermath of a bomb. 'I wonder where that one has hit' and 'They've probably bombed the Europa Hotel again.' It never seemed to register with us that lives were being lost and people were being maimed. Loss of life and livelihood was an everyday outcome of the troubles. I will never forget the 4th of November 1971. The whole school was called into the Main Hall for a 'special' morning assembly.

The mood among the staff was abnormally sombre, and our Head Teacher, Arthur G Chapman, suited in charcoal grey, blue tie and black brogues, marched in flanked by his deputies. He began abruptly by saying, 'I am afraid we have called this special assembly to bring you some bad news which will be quite shocking to hear.'

I sat waiting for an announcement of some unruly pupil's misbehaviour or some event that would have to be cancelled, or perhaps a favourite teacher was leaving, or someone had been in trouble with the law. I certainly never expected what I was about to hear.

'I am sure you all heard about the bomb in Belfast on Ormeau Road on Saturday, well I am afraid one of our teachers was an innocent victim of this latest terrorist attack. Miss Burgess was in Boyd's clothes shop where the bomb was planted. No warning was given, and Miss Burgess was there when the bomb exploded. She is now critically ill and in the Intensive care Unit at Musgrave Park Hospital, Belfast.'

The gasp around the assembly hall was audible, the shock palpable, surely not Miss Burgess. I could feel the tears welling up in my eyes, Barbara Burgess of all people, one of the teachers who had encouraged me most to stand firm as a Christian in the school. Miss Burgess, who taught me Maths and whose Christian witness, was like a beacon light of Christ for all to see. She was fighting for her life as a result of this no-warning device detonated by the IRA. Mr Chapman quickly followed up his announcement with a call to every pupil to pray for our teacher and the others injured in the Ormeau Road explosion. Three people lost their lives in this attack, but the fact that Miss Burgess's life was hanging on by a few Intensive Care lines and tubes was more shocking to us than the death toll.

The close proximity of Friends School to Belfast and the atrocity of Miss Burgess helped me to persuade Billy and Rita that I would do better and be safer as a 'day-dog' - travelling daily, thirty kilometres from Portadown to Lisburn by train.

Quaker boarding days were over at the age of sixteen, but the experience of leaving home and being alone at the age of eleven honed my character. I revelled in the persona of the wanderer, joker, and loner, but paradoxically, I had a quiet confidence that Jesus Christ was with me always. I was never alone since the day that I invited Him into my life. Spiritually, my daily routine was to start each day with prayer and a bible reading and bring the day to a close with a prayer of thanks and a plea for protection from harmful dreams, sinful thoughts, and dangers of the night.

Miss Burgess returned to Friends School on Tuesday, the 6th of June 1972. She still had a warm greeting for us when we met her between lessons, but she looked different, with facial scars and blonde hair groomed to disguise the obvious disfigurement. Five hundred stitches to her face alone took its toll visually. She walked with a hip gait that hitched and swung her prosthetic. It seemed unjust that someone with so much joy and zest for life should now be constricted to a handicap.

Her awkward walk from one school block to another looked like a major effort, and I felt so helpless as I glanced, not staring. I longed to ask, 'How is it with Jesus?' 'How do you keep the faith after your leg has been blown off?' I never dared to ask. I wanted to know if she was in pain or if she still had flashbacks from the explosion. A million questions I was afraid to pose. I had not known a disabled person first-hand before. Her Christian witness still shone through even though her body had taken a bashing. Her grit and courage, her faith and endurance were driving her on. How Barbara Burgess's determination bolstered and encouraged me in later years!

That school year, 1972/73, was the strangest of years to be living at home and commuting from Portadown to Lisburn. Aside from the train coming under frequent attack as it sped through the Kilwilkie Estate, there were Ulster Loyalist Council strikes, which brought the country to a standstill and kept school pupils at home. Not that my mother was at home that much. It was the height of Rita Burke's itinerant ministry of speaking and praying for the sick. I recorded in my diary at least ten trips abroad by the end of the year.

> Mum has been abroad four times already this year. New York, B.C. Canada, Denmark, England. Mr and Mrs Downey are staying with us again. There was a bomb scare in Miss Burgess's class today. We missed the whole of Maths lesson. We played football against Upper 6th instead. In the evening, Mr Downey gave me a lift to Hockey training at Chambers Park, Portadown.
>
> —Thursday the 15th of March 1973
>
> Mum flew to Denmark again. Mr & Mrs Downey came to stay. Went to school on train. At the end of school, there was a bomb at the train station. Blew up in front of me and DC. It was close; he was badly shocked, and his dad came for us and ran me home. I did two hours revision and then went to see Richardson's pups with Dad and Rich.
>
> —Friday the 11th of May 1973

The latter diary entry depicts the way the troubles had become part and parcel of living in Ulster in the 1970s. On that Friday, after school, I walked along Magheralave Road, downhill towards the railway footbridge, when a car bomb exploded at the station. I was within 100 metres of the train station when it went up. A plume of dust and debris rose like an expanding mushroom before my eyes. The visible eruption was followed a split second later by the boom of the explosion. An eerie silence was broken by shouting and screaming and noises of UDR and Emergency Services rushing to the scene. Amazingly, no lives were lost, a few suffered minor injuries. I milked some notoriety by claiming to be near it and seeing it first-hand, alleging to my companion 'DC' that the explosion had deafened me. In truth, I enjoyed the attention, overlooking one small matter, that it was a close call.

FOUR

Moving On

Fortified police stations, gated barriers creating control zones in towns, security searches on entering stores and random UDR vehicle checkpoints were the norm for those of us who lived in Northern Ireland in the 1970s. Then, the troubles escalated to England. On 4th February 1974, a coach transporting soldiers and civilians was bombed on the M62 Westbound, Hartshead Moor Services, and twelve people died.

It was all over the National news, and on 10th February, I was on the farm, helping my father move some cattle from here to there, and he asked, 'What do you want to study in England for? It's not safe over there. Didn't you hear the IRA bombed Parliament at Christmas, and this week there's the M62 massacre?'

'Dad, the troubles are all over the place; even the UVF are at it in Dublin now.'

'It'll break your mother's heart if you go over there. We need you to stay and work on the financial side of the business', my father pleaded, 'What's so special about Manchester anyway?'

'I can study accountancy in England and then come back and work in the business,' I countered.

Bryan Carsberg was Professor of Accountancy there. He was at the forefront of the world of corporate finance, and I wanted to study economics at his academic seat. Sir Bryan was knighted in recognition of his services to society in 1989.

'We'll never see you back here if you leave home now.'

'Look, Dad, I prayed for a place in Manchester, and I have been offered a place. So I'm believing God is in this. County Armagh will always be home to me wherever I may roam.' I was quoting a song lyric that he knew so well, and it brought a smile to his face.

I stopped short of mentioning that Manchester University was one of the leading British universities for hockey. These Godly words and worldly thoughts inspired me to accept the place offered at Manchester to study Economics, specialising in Accountancy. I was subsequently awarded a 'minimum grant' of £50 per term. Despite his protestations, my father financially supported this decision to move to England.

That final school year was a big year in several ways. At seventeen, I had progressed through the junior teams at Chambers Park, the sports stadium of Portadown Men's Hockey Club. Standing at 5'10", lithe, toned and agile, I was selected to play for Portadown's 1st X1, the youngest person to play for the senior team in the history of the club. Local media began to take an interest in my prowess.

There was another cause for curiosity: I was the first Irish goalkeeper to wear a facemask. The guard was imported from the Calgary Flames Ice Hockey team and gave me savage courage as I charged out like the fearless 'wild colonial boy' to tackle man and ball.

The Men's 1st X1 was promoted to the Premier League in my last season before leaving home. I was voted the Young Player of the Year at the end of a good season in 1974. The newspaper clips proliferated with shots of the 'masked man', and the senior Ulster selectors began to notice my exploits. I was capped for Northern Ireland (Ulster) Juniors and tipped for greater things as the season ended.

Summer wrought a change of sport to cricket. Nonetheless, I padded up once again to stand behind the stumps for Friends School 1st X1 and for Lurgan Cricket Club. For spiritual sustenance, I was a member of Ahorey Presbyterian Church, gathering each week with some two hundred farmers, country folk and workers of Burkes of Cornascriebe. I sat looking holy beside Billy Burke, who had the voice of a song thrush and the volume of a bullhorn. When the weather was good, we would head off to the caravan, perched at Peter O'Neil's by the Bloody Bridge in Newcastle. On those Sundays, we worshipped at the Elim Pentecostal Church in Newcastle, a livelier mode of veneration altogether. Weeping, extempore prayers, impromptu words from the Lord, near angelic communal singing, harmonies and all, I loved the fellowship there.

On 30th September 1974, I packed my belongings into two suitcases and boarded the 7 pm P&O Line ferry at Belfast with my brother Harry and his newlywed wife, Tricia. Father's words, 'You'll never come back,' were ringing in my ears and with a lump in my throat as we set sail for England. As we set off, I realised I hadn't even embraced my mum, dad or my ten-year-old brother Richard. As we sailed from Belfast docks, leaning over the sturdy rails on the outside deck, I blew a kiss goodbye to them, to Ulster, to the Cornascriebe tractor business and onto the wanderer's next voyage.

I thought about old friends I was leaving behind; Brian Hanna was studying at Stranmillis Teachers Training College, Belfast and 'DC' Davy Carson had chosen Coleraine's New University of Ulster. I felt like the black sheep that had fled Northern Ireland's troubles and headed for England. Out of the frying pan into the fire.

The taxi driver assured us that it always rains in Manchester as we drove from the station along Upper Brook Street to St Anselm's Hall of Residence (Slems). That would be my lodgings for the next couple of years. Two suitcases contained the sum total of my worldly possessions. On arrival, I felt like crying when I was told that I would be sharing a room for the first year. It was like going back to Ardfallen without the shoe inspection. Geraint was my roommate; his dad, a vicar, was also in the room for the double bag drop. They both seemed okay, two Welsh boyos.

I boarded an orange Selnec bus and headed down Oxford Road. Freshers week beckoned. It introduced me to Gaysoc, Custard Appreciation Society, Bonzo's Urban Spacemen, Lacrosse Club, Hang-gliders Soc, Young Conservatives, Troops Out Movement and Radio-hams Club.

Trudging from club to club in my crew-necked grey sweater and Eva-press charcoal trousers, I was beginning to think England was a strange and foreign land of weird clubs for disparate groups of peculiar people. Refreshingly, I stumbled across the Fresher's stands for MIFCU, Manchester Interfaculty Christian Union and the UAU, University Hockey Club. I duly signed up with the assurance that their reps would be in touch.

On the way back to Slems, I invested in a cheesecloth shirt, a pair of Levi's and a grey twill fabric Ex-RAF bomber jacket from Rusholm's Army and Navy Stores. Discarding the evapress kegs, I vowed to grow my ash blonde mane so that I would not stand out from the psychedelic student-crowd. The two clubs that I registered for became a spiritual and physical lifeline in those early lonesome weeks in Manchester.

Brian Rogerson looked up from the changing room bench as I walked into the University Athletic Union sports centre, The Firs.

'What are you doing here, Burkie?'

'I'm here to play hockey.'

'Welcome to Manchester; it's full of English prats who are up themselves. We'll have to show them how to play!'

Brian Rogerson played for Ulster Schoolboys with me, and we became Irish allies in the war of accents and the banter of Anglo-Irish jokes.

Training that first Thursday evening was tough. I was out of shape, and I drove myself on like a demented Pacman. I collapsed in a heap and relieved my stomach of its contents in the sand of a long jump pit. I was eager to impress my new coach and the established 1st X1 players. Every new member at training had represented a County or Country; the competition was tough.

I plucked up the courage to have a quiet word with the team coach, 'You need to know that I am a Christian, em, I go to church on Sundays, em, I don't play hockey on Sundays.'

'You might have to play on Sundays if you want to play for the University, Sonny', was his terse reply.

Back at Slems, there was a knock on my door.

'Hi, my name's Malc; I'm the MIFCU rep'. Malcolm Hyde looked more like a 1960s hippy than a Christian Union rep. He was clad in a suit of faded denim - shirt and patchwork jeans separated by a two-inch belt with an American Golden Eagle buckle. His head of shoulder-length light brown hair framed his pageboy face.

'Can I come in? Nice to meet you, Kel.'

There are quite a few Christians in Slems. We have a weekly bible reading group and a daily morning prayer time if you're interested.'

I was pleasantly surprised that Uni Christians had managed to organise themselves to meet up; 'Yeah, I'm interested, alright.'

'Good. Would you like to pray together now?'

I was taken aback by his bold request, 'All-right-ok,' I mumbled.

'You'll have to pray slower than you speak, Kel. The Lord knows what you're saying, but I can't follow a word you're saying.'

I sat on my single bed with Malc propping himself against my Olivia Newton-John poster.

He spoke to the Lord, knowing he was present with us, 'Lord, thank you for bringing my brother Kel to us. May he quickly feel a part of us because we are all part of your family, Father God, amen.'

It was a simple prayer, but I felt like I belonged after that. I had a crazy bunch of Christians who were just a door knock away, brothers in faith that I needed more often than not.

University hockey was great craic, and the standard was high. Away fixtures were quite an ordeal – spiritually. The songs we sang in high spirits often bore spiritual melodies, but the words were not from the Presbyterian Hymnal. I could sense my co-players hypocrisy radar homing in on me as they boisterously sang 'Swing Low Sweet Chariot,' 'Oh Sir Jasper,' and 'Get 'em down, you Zulu warrior.' The challenge seemed to be, can we get Kel to sing or at least smile? I confess that the humour and the laddish behaviour were part of team camaraderie, and I did not want to be a pious bore. On more than one occasion, I fought manfully as I was dragged to the back of the bus only to see my trousers head in the opposite direction. Over the years, I learnt to speak out and stand up for Jesus, and I sensed great respect from teammates as we travelled all over the country.

Big Ian, a chunky Yorkshireman from Skelmanthorpe, liked to room and travel with me on the coach.

'Kel, I know we take the p**s, but we admire you for staying true to the Christian way.'

'I couldn't betray my Lord, Ian, when I think of all he has done for me.'

'I wish I had your faith, Kel.'

'I will pray for you, Ian, and we will keep in touch. One day, you'll realise that this is the truth; it sets you free, and it gives you peace within.'

'We'll see, Kel. I think I'm a lost cause.'

By the end of the season, we were undefeated, and we had progressed to the final of the Universities Athletic Union Cup. The venue was Birmingham's Aston University. Our opponents were Bristol University.

Sidney Friskin of the Daily Telegraph was covering the final, and I scanned his sports columns to see if I got a mention. The date was set for Sunday the 14th March 1976.

Sunday! I felt numb, devastated. I phoned Ian, 'Have you heard the date.'

'Yea, I know, it's Sunday the 14th

'But I don't play sport on Sundays, Ian.'

'You'll have to play this once, Kel.'

'I can't,' I protested as I slammed the phone down. I was stunned; I phoned my mum in Portadown and asked her to pray for me. Rita hadn't taken much interest in hockey and much less in our progress to the final, but she mustered Ulster's intercessory warriors to pray that 'Kelvin would stand against this worldly temptation of Sunday sport.'

I turned to my Christian friends in Slems and asked them to pray for me, especially for wisdom concerning this UAU final.

On Thursday, 11th March, there was a knock on my door that sounded like it was being kicked in. I tentatively opened. Ian Pearson pushed past me and occupied my room.

'What's this about you not playing in the final?'

'It's on a Sunday.'

'You can't let us down, Kel. We've been together all year, and we must play the final together.'

'I wish I could Ian, I'm sorry.'

'What sort of message does this send out to our lads about your great man Jesus? We've seen what Jesus means to you, Kel, but do we mean nothing at all to you?'

'All I can say is this Ian – I'm praying about it.'

'S*d praying, you should be playing', Ian joked.' The light-hearted banter diffused the tension; we were a close-knit team, and I knew I was letting them down.

Eight students crammed into Malc Hyde's 8' x 10' bedroom for Thursday night's bible study. Mike read from the gospel of Mark Chapter 2:27, 'The Sabbath was made for man, not man made for the Sabbath.' 'Maybe this is for you, Kel,' interjected Mike. He understood the dilemma better than most. He was an Ulsterman, a sportsman and a Christian.

As a third-year mathematics student, he had worked through some of the cultural issues of a Northern Irish Protestant living in Manchester.

'Have you thought about what your teammates said to you, Kel?'

'What do you mean, Mike?'

'Well, the Gospel they are hearing is, 'thou shalt not play hockey on Sunday,' what message do you want them to hear?'

'I want them to know Jesus is more important to me than anything.'

'That's the answer, Christianity is about a person, Jesus, it's not about rules. Will these lads want to know this person, Jesus, if you walk out on them now?'

Mike's words, interwoven with Mark 2:27, gave me a new spiritual insight - I decided I would play in the final.

The rain persisted; Sunday was a grey day as we travelled by coach to Birmingham. The weather echoed my mood; I was under a cloud of guilt and questioning whether I could still claim that Christ was first in my life in the light of my Sabbath decision. As usual, Ian sat beside me on the bus. The nerves of the big occasion and my 'Sunday sin' created an uneasy tension.

The game itself was tight; we were not playing our usual passing, fast-flowing game. Bristol were pressing hard and had the better of the play.

Just before half-time, I up-ended the Bristol centre-forward without nicking the ball – penalty! The penalty flick shot past me like a bullet. We were 1-0 down at half-time. As we went off at the interval, I wondered if the Lord would punish the team for my participation. Like a modern-day Jonah, I should have been cast overboard to save the ship. The team talk was subdued as we sucked on quartered oranges. Our captain, Mark Monaghan, gave a rallying call, and we were back out for the second half.

The second half was scoreless until we were awarded a penalty corner in injury time. Mike May strode forward, crouched poised as Brian Rogerson flicked the corner to chunky Ian Pearson on his knees to hand stop. Mike's strike cracked the backboard as it flew into the right-hand corner of the goal. We were level, and the final whistle blew. The Universities Athletic Union Final was going to extra time. Our tails were up for the extra period. We went on to take the trophy, winning 2-1. The boys were euphoric, but my joy was muted. As I stared at my winner's medal, I was still unsure if the choice I had made was God-guided or worldly wisdom. My prayer was that my teammates would find faith and that they would know that Jesus Christ was more important to me than a Cup final victory.

Twenty-eight years later, I received a telephone call. A man with a Canadian accent said in Yorkshire dialect,

'Eh, up Kel, it's Ian Pearson.'

Now forty-eight years of age, he still played hockey at veterans' level. He was proud to say his son Mark, also an accomplished forward, played for Canada.

'But that's not why I am phoning, Kel.'

'So what is it, Ian?'

'Do you remember all that stuff all those years ago about Jesus and Sundays?'

'For sure.'

'Well, I wanted to tell you, I have been on one of those Alpha courses in Vancouver and I have invited Jesus into my life.'

'That's brilliant news, Ian' I exclaimed. Ian and Mark were coming over to the UK with the Canadian hockey team, and we arranged to meet up in Skelmanthorpe on 28th July 2004.

I was overjoyed by this out-of-the-blue communication from my former sport-travelling buddy. God hears and answers our prayers, sometimes not in the way we expected and sometimes after twenty-eight years, but 1 John 5:14 continues to assure me that, 'This is the confidence we have in approaching God: that if we ask anything according to his will, he hears us. And if we know that he hears us, whatever we ask, we know that we have what we asked of him.'

It was hard to knuckle down to Accountancy studies after overindulging in sport. Professor Carsberg was unimpressed by my exuberant 'we won the cup' explanations. He called me into the department before the Easter break to inquire why I was missing deadlines and failing to achieve expected grades.

His genuine threat that I should consider retaking the entire year was enough to force me to focus on my academic calling.

Five days after our UAU heroics, I was back home in Portadown for Easter, preparing for the end-of-year exams. Revision wasn't easy; there was an expectation that I ought to visit the whole family: Harry and Tricia, Grannie and Granda, aunties and uncles; Florence, Olive, Edie, Annie, Wesley and Joe, Joan and Billy. 'You should call up and see your Great Aunt Emma,' said my dad, 'and Tom Hollywood said he wants to see you.' I don't think I had ever visited Aunt Emma before, but there were lots of 'shoulds and oughts' and no interest whatsoever in Bryan Carsberg's threat.

On top of the crazy, 'Auch ye will, ye will' visiting schedule, I had to fly back to England, to Commonwealth House in London, having received an invitation from YMCA Camp Ralph S Mason in New Jersey to coach hockey for ten weeks in the summer. It was the USA's greatly anticipated Bi-Centennial year. There was a carefree part of me that thought, 'Carsberg can whistle.'

By the end of the summer term, exams done and dusted, I just had time to fly back home to Northern Ireland and pack for three months in the United States.

FIVE

Starting Out

Chris Sugden picked up the phone and rang Rev John Staley, the vicar of St Andrews Church in Wakefield. The youthful Chris, with sideburns like thatching, was one of the ministers at Holy Trinity, Platt, the church I had attended for the three University years.

Chris and John trained together in St John's Nottingham's 'vicar factory', and when he heard about my offer of work in Wakefield as an Articled Clerk for Neville Russell Chartered Accountants, he did the clergy networking 'thing' to pave the way for a 'transfer' to a new church. No money changed hands in this transaction.

I knocked on the scarlet vicarage door on Peterson Road and spoke tentatively, 'I've just moved to Wakefield, and I'm looking for a church.'

'I'm not the vicar, I'm an architect, Richard Shepley... I'm the lodger living on the top floor of the vicarage,' he answered, inviting me in.

'What's St Andrew's like?' I inquired. 'Evangelical, welcoming and growing, I just moved here from London, All Souls, Langham Place. God seems to be bringing people from all over the country to Wakefield for such a time as this.'

I was sorted; I had found a church before my first day at work and before I had found accommodation. Not to worry, I had a Ford Escort Van boarded out and enough puff to inflate an airbed in the back. That was my accommodation for the next few weeks, living out of a suitcase, knowing God had brought me to this place at the right time.

Before I arrived at College Grove, Wakefield's Hockey and Rugby Union training ground, Norman Hughes had already been described as 'Mr Wakefield Hockey.' Norman was a quietly confident man. For a British Hockey International and Wakefield's captain, he was unassuming. His physique was ideal, low centre of gravity and leg muscles like that of an ancient Greek athlete.

'If you've played for Ulster and Manchester University, we can use you,' Hughes said.

The hockey club was a family, a bit like the church without the Christ. After training, the social networking in the College Grove club bar quickly drew me in. Belonging in Wakefield was happening quick and easy.

I made my debut for Wakefield Hockey 1st X1 on 1st October 1977, a 2-2 draw with Welton. I had played well overall and set my sights on retaining my place and gaining a full international call-up. The British men's team were already preparing for the 1980 Olympic Games in Moscow, and my recurring dream was to be selected for the GB squad.

My father had heard about my housing problems and flew over from Portadown to discuss buying my own pad. He promptly placed a deposit on a house on my behalf, and I completed the deal with a mortgage. Through gritted teeth, I was grateful to accept his generosity.

I settled down to life in Wakefield; Church was good, and I was growing spiritually through St Andrew's network of house groups. Hockey was good; most of my teammates nicknamed me 'Irish' as a term of endearment. I was a regular with the 1st X1 and continued to train hard towards the 'dream' of a full senior cap for my country. Work was good; Neville Russell had an excellent graduate training programme headed by big-bearded Leonard Moore, who looked more like an Orthodox Greek prayer hermit than a Chartered Accountant. In a short time, Len had got me through my ACA professional examination, PE1.

Jane, one of the youth workers at church, accused me of being a flirt. It was really just banter to me; I was spouting Irish Blarney on all and sundry. Besides, I was falling in and out of love with Janet, my teenage sweetheart in Portadown. Furthermore, St Andrew's had a growing congregation of young, single adults, and I hung loose to many of their organised walks, picnics and day trips, but the fellowship was good.

Diary entries at this time were a running commentary on the spiritual battleground of trying to put God first in my life, and of keeping his commandments, of respecting the women I had the privilege of knowing and of not yielding to temptations.

> Went to see Janet, nice walk around Craigavon Balancing Lakes. We had a good talk about the Lord and how we didn't want our relationship to take away from God being our priority.
>
> —Sunday 7th January 1979

After twenty-two summers, life was good. I had it all: the job, the money, the sport, the detached house, the faith and the friends. What could possibly go wrong?

After passing PE 1 (part one) of the Chartered Accountancy exams, my employer pandered to my rambling 'spirit' and seconded this Irish rover to a Belfast firm in December 1978. William Fitch, senior partner of the Belfast Office, welcomed me to the Belfast team. On arrival, Armani-suited, effervescent Christian Businessman Bill said,

'I hear you're an expert in Insolvency.'

'If you say so,' I replied defensively.

'I faxed all our English offices and requested insolvency experts to help us with the McNeil Group receivership.'

'Well, the Wakefield Office sent me because I have the right accent, not because I have the right skills!'

Well, you have passed PE1; you should be good enough. You're in charge of Portadown Foundry and Ballinderry Concrete,' Fitch conceded.

'Two companies?'

'That's right, two.'

I was in at the deep end of the insolvency business, and I didn't even know the difference between a liquidation and a receivership! I soon learnt! The Receiver keeps the company trading, endeavouring to dispose of the venture as a going concern.

At the age of twenty-two, part qualified and novice-green in insolvencies, I was heading up two Limited Companies with two Managing Directors answering to me! I felt like a duck floating serenely on the water but paddling like billy-o underneath. This was one situation where the staff and prospective purchasers would see straight through my Blarney. My prayers were short and sweet, 'Lord, help me.' 'Lord, grant me wisdom beyond my years.'

That first morning's bible reading from Isaiah 41:10 spoke to me like an audible word of the living God, 'Fear not for I am with you, be not dismayed for I am your God. I will strengthen you, yes, I will help you, I will uphold you with my righteous right hand.'

It felt like God was upholding me; the two Managing Directors, Pat and Gordon, gave me undeserved and unreserved respect. The staff in the companies grafted for the short-term future of their firms, and my regular meetings with the workforce created a team spirit that belied my inexperience.

It was good to be back with Ahorey Presbyterians, too. Eileen Marshall, proprietor of the Christian book shop in Portadown, invited me to speak at the midweek meeting at Ahorey Presbyterian Church. A couple of dozen sat reverently; among them were my old Sunday School teachers, Tommy Foster and Edmund Greer, Miss Marshall, Miss Gordon and twenty others. All eagerly leafing through their leather-bound bibles as I taught these 'teachers' from Luke 18:1-8, Jesus' parable to show us that we 'should always pray and not give up.' It was a minor meeting in the grand scheme of things, but somehow, I felt it was significant, like a preparation of some sort. I wrote in my diary:

> Spoke at a meeting in Ahorey – I felt the Lord guide my words, I didn't feel nervous. Spoke on Luke 18 – praise God…..this is another step in ministering for the Lord. I don't feel capable, inadequate even, but barriers have been broken down tonight.

—Tuesday 30th January

One of my duties as Receiver was to negotiate the sale of my two companies as going concerns. On Wednesday, 31st January, I sat in Bill Fitch's plush offices in downtown Belfast, waiting nervously for prospective purchasers W.D. Irwin and their solicitor. The door opened, and leading solicitor Brian Walker breezed in, followed by two of Irwin's directors. Brian's ginger afro hair matched his eccentric 'take no prisoners' style of negotiating, and I should have been quaking at the sight of him. Except for one minor detail - he was a second cousin of mine, and we hadn't met since I was an eight-year-old apple tree climber.

In a moment of foolish familiarity, I introduced myself to WD Irwin's directors, saying I had attended school with the Irwin children and turning to Walker, I said, 'Brain, I am a relative of yours, long time no see!'

The solicitor opened a battered buff file and barked;

'Young man, has this meeting started yet? My clients are busy men, and we haven't come here to be nostalgic!'

I rocked back on my boardroom chair, grasping hopelessly for some of the wisdom I had prayed for that morning. Irwins had come to acquire my company, and I had revealed my inexperience in Receivership negotiations.

I survived the mauling, and, in the end, the outcome for all parties was favourable. We accepted their offer and set up the creditors meeting and a completion date in April.

I returned to England for a couple of weeks in March. On 30th March 1979, there was breaking news of Airey Neave's assassination. Neave was Northern Ireland spokesman for Margaret Thatcher's Conservatives, and his untimely death at the hands of the INLA (Irish National Liberation Army) was a sharp reminder to me of the escalating troubles throughout the United Kingdom. The McNeil experience had been a positive one as an accounting adventure, and I wondered if I should return home to settle in Northern Ireland. My roots in Wakefield were shallow and revolved around St Andrew's Church, Wakefield Hockey Club and a desire to see the Chartered Accountancy studies through to ACA qualification. Nonetheless, as I flew back to Belfast on Easter Tuesday, 17th April, for the Portadown Foundry creditors meeting, it felt like a homecoming. It turned out to be a brush with death.

The taxi from Aldergrove Airport dropped me at Duncrue Street, the headquarters of the McNeil Group. I intended to do some last-minute preparation for the meeting on the 18th. Gerry, the security guard on entry, welcomed me home and said that I would be lucky to see anyone in the offices. 'It's the day after the bank holiday, Kelvin; most of us have taken the week after Easter off.'

'But we have an important meeting tomorrow.'

'It may be important for you, but if your company is going bust, you would rather be with your family; that's more important.'

I walked on in and settled down in the deserted Accounts office, sifting through folders and files, fact-finding in preparation for the Creditor's meeting. The whole complex was like a ghost town; I could imagine tumbleweed drifting by outside. In reality, most of the information I needed was locked in cabinets or stored in memory banks in the brains of staff who were enjoying an extended Easter break. Gerry's words echoed back at me, 'The family is more important.'

At 2.30 pm, after a fruitless hour in the McNeil offices, I stood up, stuffed a few papers in my briefcase and decided to catch the train to Portadown to spend Easter time with my family. Gerry was right.

My mother was surprised to see her middle son walk through the door at 4.30 pm. I had not warned her that I was travelling back to the province.

'Have you heard about the explosion?' Rita exclaimed.

'What explosion, mum? I've been in Belfast, and I heard nothing.'

'There was an explosion at the headquarters of the McNeil Group.'

I rushed to the TV to catch the evening news, 'There was an explosion at 3 pm at the main offices of the McNeil Group, which is in receivership. No one was injured, but the damage is extensive.'

I could feel my face draining of colour. I had been in those offices a half hour before, and if Gerry hadn't spoken about 'family time', I would have been working there at the time of the explosion. The report continued, 'The bomb was hung on the outside wall of the pre-fabricated offices at Duncrue Street.' The offices where I had sat until 2.30 pm. Providentially, God had moved me to get a move on. I thanked the Lord for nudging me to go home through the words of an angel in the guise of security guard Gerry Malone.

I returned to Wakefield a week later, certain that God's sovereign hand was upon my life. I was less certain of where I should settle, Ireland or England. My family was in Portadown, but my Christian family was in both Yorkshire and Ulster. Little did I know I would soon have to make a life-defining choice that would root me in one of those camps.

SIX

Honister

The Full Gospel Businessmen's Breakfast on 12th May 1979 was electrifying. More than a hundred of us squeezed into the banqueting hall at the new Novotel in Bradford. Sports Physio, Jim accompanied me in consuming a 'Full English' before the main speaker, balding Bob Spillman, stood to 'give a word.' He was the National President of FGBUK and took from Romans 8:14-17 the theme, 'You are the Children of God,' interjecting with testimony of how the Heavenly Father had been faithful throughout his life from Nigeria and Ghana to Knutsford in Cheshire. There was a special something, an anointing, as he spoke, especially as he expounded Romans 8:16, 'The Spirit himself testifies with our spirit that we are God's children.' 'Imagine a courtroom drama', he said, 'you are a child of God, that is your testimony. Your accuser says you are not. Then the Holy Spirit takes the stand and testifies with you and for you - yes, it is true, you are a child of God. Everyone in that courtroom is convinced now - the Spirit testifies in your defence - it is tremendous assurance, a powerful defence.'

Something registered deep within me that was precious, 'I am a child of God,' I felt an overwhelming joy bubbling up within my soul. I knew this before; I had been taught it for a dozen years, from Sunday School to the Presbyterian pulpits. On this day, a couple of weeks short of my 23rd birthday, I felt secure in this blessed assurance. I was overwhelmed like Peter in 1 Peter 1:8 with a 'joy unspeakable and full of glory.'

> Hallelujah, what a great day of praising and learning about the Lord. Went to FGBMFI Breakfast in Bradford. Cheshire's Bob Spillman spoke well – 'We Are children of God.' He prayed with me when I spoke to him afterwards. The Lord gave me a word. In the evening, Jim and I had a special time of prayer.
>
> —Saturday 12th May 1979

The near miss of the McNeil bomb scare brought it home to me that I am one of God's own, adopted, known, and loved. My life is in his hands, not the terrorist's roll of a dice. God providentially kept me from harm on that day in Belfast. Twenty-five days later, in a hotel in Bradford, 'the Spirit testified with [my] Spirit that [I] am a child of God' (Romans 8:16). I sensed that the Lord was preparing me in some way for something. It was subliminal, but when I looked back to my pensive reflection on New Year's Day 1979, I had written, unknowingly prophetically;

> 'I don't know what the year ahead holds for me, there will be some surprises, I believe my hockey will be affected, maybe something to do with my legs.'
>
> —1 January 1979

It is incredible that my musing as I 'stood at the gate of the year' should emphasise 'surprises ahead' because of what transpired five months later. If we commit our 'way' to God, though we do not have insight into the future, I am convinced He prepares us for challenges and difficulties ahead.

Four months later, on Saturday 12th May 1979, after the FGB breakfast, I wrote; 'Who knows what the Lord has in store? Who needs to? I just need to trust and obey; that's all I can say, I'm secure in Jesus, He leads the way.'

My next accounting duties took me to the South Lakes to audit a company in Lancaster. One balmy summer's night, after work, I tootled along the A590 to Newby Bridge on the southern tip of Lake Windermere. Sat alone, drinking in the vista of the surrounding peaks, the fast-flowing Leven and gently sloping wooded hills, my appetite was well and truly whetted for a week of hiking in the Lake District with St Andrew's young adults.

The flow of traffic on Friday, 25th May, on the A65, was hectic. The drive across the Pennines from White Rose to Red Rose County is a rich mixture of bleak purple heathered ridges and lush sheep-dotted valleys and streams. Despite the awesome beauty, the road from Keighley to Settle was tedious in the bank holiday traffic.

A stop-off for hydration at the spectacular twin-arched Devil's Bridge at Kirkby Lonsdale was timely. Kayakers lazed on the rocks, and children skimmed flat stones on the River Lune. It was an idyllic gateway to the Lake District. We were relieved to cross the single-arched granite Grange bridge over the River Derwent in Borrowdale and arrive in the stunning hamlet of Grange at dusk.

Richard Shepley, my roommate for the expedition, had arrived earlier and erected our two-man tent at the St Andrew's base camp on the local farm and campsite by the banks of the river. David was acting camp commandant, and his wife Mary had a 'billy' on the campfire for the evening's hot chocolate for late arrivals and drifters such as me.

Later, when the base camp was set, we perched on tree stumps around the fire, and all was well. There was peace and quiet at the end of the day, a perfect start to our St Andrew's trip. We hit the canvas after a quick prayer; the expedition was up and running.

Each evening brought the group together after individual sorties into the Lakes. Campfire stories were told of excursions to Keswick and Derwentwater, Grasmere and Wordsworth's Cottage at Ambleside. Commandant Dave led an expedition up Skiddaw, which I opted out of, preferring to bask in the Bank Holiday sun and swim in the river lapping metres from our camp. My blue pocket-size Bible, awarded in 1964 for 'Good Attendance' at Ahorey Sunday School, was well-leafed as I reflected on the beauty around me. The sound of crystal-clear flowing waters, tranquil wooded meadows and distant buzzards was the perfect antidote to the world of insolvency and audit that had preceded this retreat.

Sat on riverbank boulders with tears in my eyes, I recited the words of Psalm 42 to express my yearning for God;

> 'As a deer longs for the flowing streams, so my
> soul longs for you, O God.'

This Lakeland farmstead took me back to the good, arable Armagh countryside I grew up in. I felt like I was one with creation, the oak woodland, the grazing sheep and the Friesian cattle surrounded by high fells. 'Let the rivers clap their hands and the mountains sing for joy before the Lord' (Psalm 98:8). The trip was becoming a special oasis, recharging my spiritual batteries, feasting on bible readings and prayer times and drinking in the stunning Lake District scenery.

On 30th May, the St Andrew's camp commune decided to embark on a group activity. We would drive to Buttermere

Lake and climb Buttermere Fell to the 2417-foot summit of Robinson and cross the ridge to Hindscarth with excellent views down Honister Pass.

I wandered back from my morning riverbank prayer time, having read Psalm 27: 'The Lord is my light and my Salvation; whom shall I fear.' I underlined verse 4, 'One thing I have asked of the Lord, that I will live in the house of the Lord all the days of my life, to behold the beauty of the Lord… for He will hide me in his shelter in the day of trouble.' As I prayed and read the scriptures, I sensed an assurance that the Lord knew my desire to be committed to Him, and I knew his promise was true: I would 'be sheltered in the day of trouble.'

Eleven of us, in two cars, set out for Buttermere. *Alan's 1964 Morris was overloaded with five adults and baby Ben in a carrycot. Honister Pass was an ordeal for the Morris Minor Traveller. The steep 1:3 inclines and bends are a challenge to any motorist, but the fifteen-year-old Morris laboured up the steep inclines until we arrived at our roadside destination on the outskirts of Buttermere village.

The craic was good up the fellside; I was determined to exhibit above-average fitness levels and thus tackled the ascent in poll position. The rucksacked six-month-old Ben was laid on my shoulders. I enjoyed being a beast of burden for the infant up Robinson Fell. From the 737-metre summit, there were spectacular views of Crummock Water in the South and the sheer face of Fleetwith Pike and Honister Craig, a playground for adrenaline junkies and experienced rock climbers. We trekked north along Robinson's plateau and paused to absorb the breathtaking views of Newlands Valley and beyond to Derwent water fornent our campsite. We sat in near silence, devouring our sandwiches, admiring the fine Lakeland panorama, and inwardly praising our creator God. Baby

HONISTER

Ben screamed as five Tornado Jets pierced the silence with supersonic destruction, flying below us along the valley on an RAF training exercise. We took the jet's cue to arise and make our descent along the slate-strewn path back to Buttermere.

I expected and sought some praise or acclamation for being the first back to the cars. None was forthcoming; the exhausted trekkers talked of primroses and buttercups, crystal streams and stone-walled fields, but there was no acknowledgement that I was first and the fittest! Nonetheless, there was weary contentment and a communal feeling that we had achieved something at the end of a special day.

Five adults, me and Alan, Sue, Diane, Sarah and baby Ben, squeezed like sardines into Alan's Morris as we set off after Dave's vehicle up Honister Pass. This mountain pass is not for the fainthearted motorist. At times, the front of the car juts out over the brow of the hill and blocks the view of the road ahead. Every driver makes a heart-stopping guess that the road is straight ahead.

Honister climbs at 1 in 3 with a metre-high stone wall curb on one side and a sheer drop to Gatesgarthdale Beck on the other.

We were in good spirits heading back to base camp at Grange. Sue launched into a Fisher-Folk chorus, and four joined in impromptu praise. Alan's Morris Traveller groaned under the people-load and the steep gradient. Suddenly, within twenty metres of Honister's summit, the Morris' engine stalled. I instinctively flicked off my seat belt, opened my door and said, 'We've all got to get out and push.' Alan stamped his left boot on the clutch, and the vehicle shot back at a frightening speed. I looked sideways at Alan; he was frantically trying to break and control the steep descent.

In desperation, he yanked the hand break up but lost control of the Morris reversing, freewheeling down the 1 in 3, and we careered into the unforgiving stone wall on the passenger side. The open door was ripped off in the impact, and the car hurtled backwards towards the bank on the other side of the road.

There was a moment of immobility as the car balanced like a fulcrum on the bank's edge. I held onto the doorframe and leant outwards to add weight to the up-side of the car as it see-sawed on the bank. It seemed to work for a second or two, and then it went, tumbling out of control, somersaulting down the steep gorge towards Gatesgarthdale Beck. The sound of glass breaking and metal scraping and ripping was deafening; the girls were screaming, and baby Ben was screaming, too. I was tossed like a rag doll from the passenger's seat and into the path of the Morris as it wrote itself off down the ravine.

I regained consciousness in a dazed sensation of watery confusion. There was a silent stillness. I was in the beck, pinned beneath the Morris. Conscious of the fast-flowing stream but totally helpless, unable to move or breathe or speak. The sill of the Morris was across my back. I could do nothing but wait for help.

It wasn't long before motorists from the road above and climbers from Honister Crag rushed to my aid. A doctor in a passing car scrambled down the steep embankment and administered first aid, directing operations in a desperate attempt to save my life.

Six strong climbers formed a human 'jack' and hulked the Morris off my crushed frame.

'Now, crawl out!' Alan yelled.

I commanded the legs that had just conquered Robinson Fell into action.

There was no response. I was utterly taken aback, the head dictated, and the legs disobeyed. I clawed at the water, desperate to help myself from underneath the Morris before submitting to my incapacity. I lay motionless. The strain was beginning to break the 'car-lifters.'

Diane urged, 'Kel, quick, crawl out to the bank.'

I tried to muster the legs into action once again, but they were two paralysed limp limbs, behaving as if they belonged to another person, no movement, just numb like battle-weary AWOL deserters.

I tried to reply to Diane to explain the dilemma. My attempt at words was equally fruitless; the Blarney-meister was silenced, and no sound came out despite my efforts to speak. Once again, I submitted again to the helplessness.

Two bystanders crawled into the stream and cradled me from the elevated vehicle.

The Doctor on duty issued instructions to minimise damage to the spine. I was laid vertical on the steep bank. My legs crumbled below me, the heels unable to dig into the steep incline. Dave Gardner held me by the shoulders and spoke sound-bite words of comfort.

'You're safe now, Kel.'

'The ambulance is on its way.'

'Everyone's praying for you, Kel, hang in there.'

I prayed inwardly and desperately,

'Lord, don't let me die here, don't let me die now, Lord, I'm too young to die, Lord let me live. Lord, I want to do much more in my life, Lord, I want to do more for you.'

My prayer was a barrage of desperate pleas; my eyes looked beyond the rugged rock of Honister Crag to my almighty hope, my rock of ages. I knew I was fading; all around, the people, the slopes, the bright sunlight were fading from colour to grey and then to dark - blind. I felt cold and distant, conscious that my breathing was insufficient but unable to improve on the previous breath. It was like being winded in a sporting collision, but it wasn't easing.

Curate Ron knelt beside me, crouching over me, praying softly, audibly in my left ear. He assured me, 'The Lord is with you. Do you feel his presence, Kel?'

I winced as I shook my aching head negatively; I could taste blood in my mouth; my teeth had pierced my bottom lip. I thought, 'Ron is a clown.' In my darkest hour, he asks if I feel the Lord is here! No, I do not feel the Lord is here!

Then, at that instant, what sounded like an audible voice spoke to me, 'I am with you, always.' These five words echoed like a heartbeat, over and over again, 'I am with you always.' I recognised them as the last words of Jesus to his followers, and I began to say his name in my head: Jesus, Jesus, Jesus, Jesus. I was holding on to the rock, and as I mantra'd that beautiful name, it was like ointment to my broken soul. And the pulse, 'I am with you, always,' continued to answer the name I whispered, strengthening me for the next feeble breath, driving me on to survive.

I could hear a siren in the distance, taking forever to get across the mountain pass to my aid. The Doctor handed over to the paramedics and I was strapped in and 'stretchered' up the steep incline and into the waiting ambulance. Oxygen was like sweet nectar to my collapsed lungs. I continued to fight for every breath as we sped towards Whitehaven's West Cumberland Hospital. I was able to whisper two words, 'How long?'

'We'll be there in ten minutes,' replied the paramedic.

I asked for a fourth time, and I managed a smile as he repeated the same 'ten minutes' for the last time.

The vehicle stopped, and I was rushed into the theatre for emergency surgery. The laparotomy for the internal bleeding, a rib had pierced my lung. Recovering in the ICU, the winded feeling began to subside, and I was able to speak again.

The Doctor was diligently 'testing' my legs. There was no response to the reflex test or the pain test, and I could not perform any voluntary leg movement.

The Doctor spoke to me like he was on the film set of 'Casualty.'

'Mr Burke, we have examined the X-ray of your spine, and I am sorry to tell you, on impact, the car crushed your eleventh and twelfth Thoracic vertebrae. There is no longer a gap between these vertebrae, and your spinal cord has been severed. You are paralysed from the waist down and are unlikely to regain sensation or to walk again.'

I replied gently but confidently to the medic, 'I will walk again.'

I felt faith rising within me, and I began to pray for help from my rock, Jesus. I understood the permanency of his prognosis, but I was determined to re-channel the energy I exerted in sport to my rehabilitation. From that moment, I believed that with God's help and hard work, I would recover and I could walk again.

Mum, Dad and Harry arrived the following day and visited me in Whitehaven's Intensive Care Unit. A nurse was monitoring my recovery. Mum was 'laying on hands' constantly praying, crying out to the Lord for a miracle healing, Dad and Harry looking on, silently interceding.

Post-operation, I was stitched like a zip fastener from my sternum to the belly button. Less than twenty-four hours after surgery, I had to make a decision that would affect the rest of my life. I was barely able to string a sentence together in conversation when 'Dr Kildare' asked my parents to leave as he pulled the curtains around my domain.

'Since you are over twenty-one, you must make this choice alone. He continued, 'We have emergency beds waiting for you in Wakefield and Belfast. You will be in rehabilitation for several months. Where do you wish to be hospitalised?'

What a choice! Wakefield had been my home for just twenty months, and Northern Ireland had been my home for twenty years before University. Billy and Rita were distraught that I chose Pinderfield's Hospital in Wakefield as my lodgings for the rest of the year. Like a sapling tree, I had put down tender roots there; Christian fellowship, my accountancy, and Wakefield Hockey Club were in the equation. On the other hand, I could be mollycoddled in Ulster for the foreseeable future. It was actually no contest; I knew I had to do this alone, me and the Lord, hard graft and prayer. I could fully rely on God, or I could fully rely on others, FROG or FROTH. I chose the road less travelled.

On Friday, the first of June, I was flown by military helicopter to Pinderfields Hospital accompanied by my 'Nightingale' nurse, who had hand-held me, sat by my bedside and reassured me throughout the three-day Intensive Care. She was a lifesaver. I was given a Police and Ambulance escort to the Spinal Injuries Unit. A crowd gathered around the landing area, and cameras clicked.

My first diary entry after the accident read;

> Flown to Wakefield by helicopter, lot of attention and photographs, Police, Ambulance, Fire Engine, the lot! I felt like one of the Osmonds.
>
> —1 June 1979

I was back at home in Wakefield. Let the rehabilitation begin!

SEVEN

Learning to Walk Again

Pinderfield's Spinal Injury Unit (SIU) was 'home' for most of my twenty-third year. Straddled horizontally over a dense foam support for eight weeks, I pondered what the future held when everything in the garden had seemed rosy in May. The first hurdle was to knit and fuse the broken eleventh and twelfth vertebrae. It wasn't the best of birthday presents. Immediately, auditing and professional accountancy exams were put on hold, hockey was scratched, flirtatiousness was annulled, and my new two-storey house was home to friends and family visiting from Ireland and elsewhere! Mentally and emotionally, I recoiled within myself, choosing to be quiet. The blarney-boy became a man of few words, but inwardly, I was desperate to walk again. My heart was breaking with the thought that I could do nothing to change my paralysis. I felt a determination welling within me to regain upper-body strength and learn to walk again in some form or another.

Coupled with that inner drive was an acceptance that the

Whitehaven doctor was right. My spinal cord was severed; there was no medical operation or treatment and no amount of rehabilitation that would enable the spinal cord to find a way through or around the crushed vertebrae. There was no way my brain could get a message through to my legs, not even to twitch a toe! As I lay arched backwards in the acute wing of Ward F1, counting ceiling tiles and sideways observing fellow 'paras' at varying stages of rehabilitation, I struggled mentally with losing mobility.

Like a sin-binned sportsman, I lay passive, wishing I was active – shackled by arm drips, nose and mouth tubes, a bladder cannula and to add insult to injury, I was dependent on nurses, fork-feeding and, when it was my turn, the embarrassment of bed-bathing.

Ward F1 seemed to operate a 'cruel to be kind' philosophy. The Bald Eagle – charge nurse, Ron Mullins, ruled his ward like the Governor of Wakefield's High-Security prison. Attention and affection seemed to be in short supply in keeping with the ward's philosophy. It taught fledgling paraplegics to fend for themselves, subconsciously striving for independence. On the other hand, my mum and dad, who were now residing at my house in Wakefield, were encamped at my bedside, lovingly reacting to my every cough and whimper. Communication between staff and family was brusque as one failed to grasp the others' philosophy.

Fellow patients who had progressed through the 'acute' stage to the scooting-around-in-a-wheelchair stage would stop by my bed and knowledgeably assure me, 'It's awful for the next two months, and then it gets better.' I could see the benefit of waiting a couple of months before passing on such knowledge. Nonetheless, their predictions were accurate; the first weeks brought periods of constant sickness, severe abdominal and back pain, burst stitches, minor operations, X-rays and IVPs, DVTs (Deep Vein Thrombosis) and UTIs (Urinary Tract Infections), a virus, and temperatures fluctuating up to 104°F

Despite these setbacks and suffering, my faith was buoyed by Christ's words to me on Honister's steep bank, 'I am with you always.' The blue-backed pocket Bible presented in 1964 by Ahorey Presbyterian Sunday School survived the accident and was now my daily resource in Ward F1, Pinderfields. Each day, a verse or a paragraph would stand out as my 'word for the day.' A couple of times per week, the Hospital Chaplain, Rev Roger, would 'pop by' and we would swap 'thoughts-for-the day,' pray together and share Holy Communion as brothers in Christ. Spiritually, it was a special time despite the hardship. Visits from Rev. John Staley, Rev Alan Bain, and friends at St Andrew's Church and visits from Christian friends across the UK and Ireland encouraged me to endure and to stand firm. This accident was big news in the local Christian community, and I sensed God's family united through prayer and pain shared.

Word had gone out through my mother and father's global network of praying Christians, 'Rita Burke's son had been paralysed in a car accident; please pray for a miracle.' Across the USA, from Oral Roberts Prayer Tower in Tulsa to Francis McNutt's prayer team in Florida and in Canada, from Pastor Ern Baxter's church in Vancouver to Pastor Ben Crandall's International Christian Centre (ICC) in New York, Rita Burke's son was 'lifted up' in prayer. Similarly, in Europe, Denmark in particular, the prayer request was conveyed, and my spiritual mentors Denis Clark and Alex Buchanan urged 'Intercessors for Britain' to pray. If ever the ground was prepared for a spectacular miracle to defy the world of medicine, this was it.

I felt surrounded by 'walls of prayer' as I lay in F1's acute ward in those early weeks. My diary reflects the practical struggle with the paraplegia and the spiritual struggle to praise and glorify God despite the circumstances, agreeing with St Paul, who said, 'I have learnt wherever I am to be content.'

> Today, I have had a rather hard time, but God is victorious in these situations. First, I had a minor operation to insert a cannula, a bit painful but a good Doctor. In the evening, the sausage roll was a bad idea. I was sick six times; Mum and Tricia got it on them four times! Had a few visitors but I wasn't in good form to talk to them.
>
> —Monday 11th June 1979
>
> Today was a better day, helped by a few nice letters and cards. I generally found a peace in the Lord by praising him and thinking of verses of scripture, 1 Peter 1:6 and Isaiah 58:8. I feel a bit of pain in the spine but it wasn't able to break my spirit. Good to see some visitors, it's exciting to see the way God is working in other people's lives through this accident.
>
> 1 Peter 1:6-7 'In this you rejoice, even if now for a little while you have had to suffer various trials, so that the genuineness of your faith, being more precious than gold that is tested by fire, may be found to result in praise and glory and honour when Jesus Christ is revealed.'
>
> Isaiah 58:8 'Your light shall break forth like the dawn, and your healing shall spring up quickly; your vindicator shall go before you, the glory of the Lord shall be your rearguard.'
>
> —Tuesday 12th June 1979
>
> Woke up with a heavy head and pain in my sinuses, quite uncomfortable. I felt lethargic and just dozed all day. My temperature shot over 102°F, and they put a fan on me. At times like this, it's difficult to meditate on the Word. I can but mechanically praise God and hope that He is blessed by these praises. Sue came and prayed with

me; gave a prophecy assuring me of God's guidance and healing. Praise Him.

—Wednesday 13th June 1979

Rough night's sleep, severe pains in my stomach. Vomited in the morning and again at dinner and later. I think they have diagnosed a virus in my tummy. I feel very weak. It's hard to praise God in this weakness but I have found a victory in praying in the spirit and comfort from Psalm 33. Clarence hitch-hiked from Ireland to visit me, good to see him.

—Saturday 16th June 1979

One strange outcome of the intensity of a disabling injury is the misconception that the world has stopped while the patient suffers. I had little thought for what was going on beyond Pinderfield's Spinal Unit. My focus was on me and my predicament, and I cared little for world affairs or even Wakefield's news. Visits from friends and family helped me to regain perspective and stay connected to the community 'out there.'

The assets and fixtures from The McNeill Group went under the auctioneer's hammer in Belfast at the end of June, and a cheery phone call with Peter and Iaon on the Receivership team reminded me of the good work that had gone on there in the first six months of the year. It brought closure to the work I began in January 1979.

There was another kind of closure too. In these early weeks of hospitalisation, I made a difficult decision to end my relationship with my girlfriend from Northern Ireland, Janet. We had been seeing each other, on and off, for a couple of years, and she had recently moved to London, England. We both thought we would see more of each other, that was before 30th May 1979. As I lay bedridden in those early weeks, I couldn't get it out of my head that I did not want to put anyone else through this trauma. I would do it alone, me and Jesus, but the thought of having a girlfriend who would have to face the difficulties of a boyfriend who was now a paraplegic, troubled me. Janet was a special Christian girl who played hockey for Portadown Ladies First XI. We had farming, faith and sport in common.

Now, as I lay staring at the ceiling in Pinderfields Spinal Injuries Unit, I was overthinking what my future may look like post-recovery. Some of the Job's comforters who visited me had advised that I would not be able to have children. Consequently, I could not fathom how my future relationships would involve anything other than platonic friendships. Janet graciously accepted my hasty call as I prepared myself for the months of rehabilitation and lifelong celibacy.

Visits from Neville Russell work colleagues assured me there was work to go back to and that the 'Irish wit' was being missed in the office. A Christian friend and work colleague, Sally, called in and gave me quadriplegic Joni Eareckson's life story and then dropped a bombshell that she had just been diagnosed with terminal cancer. Sally and I started at Neville Russell on the same day in 1977. Now, at the age of twenty-three, both of our lives had been turned upside down, and she was dealing with a different challenge. Sally died before she could complete her final PE 2 Chartered Accountancy exams in 1980. These 'moments of reality' helped me regain perspective, that my struggles were just that - 'struggles' - which were surmountable with the help of God, in time and in eternity.

I began to appreciate that the Hospital Chaplain's pastoral visits and sharing Holy Communion together, coupled with those of St Andrew's friends, were nourishing me with fellowship, rooting me in the community that I had been temporarily forced out of for a period, to recuperate and rehabilitate.

The 'worst' two months ended on 28th July 1979, the day Pinderfield's Doctor Rainey, an Ulsterman, declared me fit to be transferred into a wheelchair. The long days of counting F1's polystyrene ceiling tiles were over. The vertebrae had healed and fused, as had the stitches in my abdomen. However, the ordeal of progressing from lying flat to sitting in a wheelchair was more complicated than I imagined. It was the first time that I truly realised what it felt like to be paralysed. Lying in the bed, I had no sensation below the waist, but I had no idea what that meant to my balance, my mobility or my mind. My diary records the 'moment:'

> Got up before dinner. It is the weirdest and most shocking experience I think I have come across.
>
> Firstly, male nurse Maurice lifted me onto my bum on the edge of the bed. I think that was the worst bit. The shock of knowing I had nothing below the waist, no feeling, no movement, no control, nothing. I started praying in the spirit and praising the Lord, and when Maurice put me in the wheelchair and wheeled me to the outside door for fresh air, I felt comforted.
>
> All at once, the room started to go dark. I couldn't see, but I could hear. I felt like I couldn't speak and started to pass out; I came too when they tipped the chair back. Next, I started to shake uncontrollably; after a while, I began to feel better and was able to propel the chair by myself, which seemed to surprise a few. Richard and Mum came later, and I tried to play table tennis against Richard (my younger brother). Sally from work came with a book and presents from our Southport Office.
>
> —Saturday 28th July 1979

After the weekend, Physio Roger Ellis was eagerly waiting

in the SIU gym. Roger followed the same philosophy as the Bald Eagle with a slight sadistic twist.

'OK, Kelvin, we'll start with the plinth. Transfer from your wheelchair, push off with your left arm and land close to your right hand. You should be strong enough, unless you're a weakling, of course.'

My left and right arms guided my body onto the plinth, and Ellis knelt behind me. I thought he was supporting me from falling backwards. My balance was wobbly. I felt like I was rocking on an oily ball bearing. Without sensation in my legs or bottom, balance had to be gained by taking sight lines. 'This may hurt a bit,' the physio crouched over my shoulders and pushed my head forward towards my numb limbs.

'Easy on there, Rog, I've already had my back broken once,' I cried.

'We have to do this to stretch your hamstrings; they've tightened over the last eight weeks,' he pushed again; my forehead was touching my knees, sweat fell from my brow, and the pain was both excruciating and exhausting.

'You should be able to kiss the plinth between your legs by the time we've finished.'

> Went into the gym and into Roger's hands, quite an ordeal on the plinth. Did some weights, played table tennis, they were impressed – I wasn't. It's hard to accept that you can't play some strokes as before because of the wheelchair. I've started to act the wag a bit. It's a long time since I felt full of beans.
>
> Later, John Staley visited, had good prayer time with him. Encouraged by Hebrews 12:11, 'discipline always seems painful…but later it yields the peaceful fruit of righteousness.'

LEARNING TO WALK AGAIN

—Monday 30th July 1979

Felt good this morning, got up early, went to the gym and did a wee spell on the plinth and did some weights. Felt tired at dinnertime and Harry and Tricia had to help me to bed at 4 pm. Then sickness hit me. High-Temperature 104°F, then I puked a bucket full. They called the doctor; I was panicking - breathing problems, going for a chest X-ray tomorrow.

—Tuesday 31st July 1979

Headache was almost unbearable this morning, seemed to be poker hot, soaking wet and my neck in such pain. I was in rigours and temperature was 103°F. My forehead was so heavy. Felt like I had a brick over my right eye. Several people visited, but I had no chat. I really want to be off this drip, I can't use my left arm.

—Thursday 2nd August 1979

Harry and Tricia came in the morning and then went to Nostell Priory. I felt a good deal better today; the heaviness is leaving, and for the first time, I really thought about the Lord in this bout of sickness.

I had prayed to be healed, but my faith couldn't compete with the pain. Dave and Mary Gardner came and prayed for me. Slept till 2 am then woke and had a good time of prayer and thoughts about the future and many things. The Lord gave me sleep as dawn broke. Glory.

—Friday 3rd August 1979

After the setback of the UTI (Urinary Tract Infection), I was back in the gym, ready for more Roger Ellis pounding. Ever since the Whitehaven medic told me I would never walk again, I had dreamt of proving him wrong. I know he meant walking unaided, with legs that obeyed head-sent instructions, but I had discussed walking with callipers to Phil Taylor, the Orthotist, and my upper body strength was improving daily. I felt my upper body was ready to step up to the plate and do the work my legs refused to do.

> Got up, had a bath – it's hard to balance on my bum! Had a mini quiet time, read 1 Peter 5:10 'and after you have suffered a little while, the God of all grace who has called you to his eternal glory in Christ, will himself restore, establish and strengthen you.'
>
> Went in gym and onto the plinth. Roger almost killed me. Terrible pain as he pushed me further, but it's the end product that matters. Went back in gym in afternoon and did weights for upper body. Listened to Dales Bible Week tape of worship – very good.
>
> —Monday 6th August 1979

> Stood up for the first time since 30th May. Put on full-length leg callipers and I stood up in parallel bars and did some balancing exercises.
>
> In the evening, Harry and Tricia took me home to my house. Great to be home, had tea there. Nice atmosphere, praised God and sang along with Fisherfolk music.
>
> —Tuesday 7th August 1979

> Did some weights in the morning, an Olympic Trainer for weightlifting was coaching me. I walked on callipers for the first time this afternoon. I went to the Hospital Chapel afterwards and had a time of prayer and worship. I wish I was a bit more spiritual. I'm getting into a sort of routine in Hospital now, and the Lord doesn't seem to feature as much. But today I walked, glory be to God.
>
> —Thursday 9th August 1979

Seventy days after my Honister Horror, I stood up and looked at my carers eye to eye. Sure, I was totally dependent on full-length leg callipers, locked at the knee, but it felt good to stand and even better to walk a few steps a couple of days later. I knew this wasn't the physical healing that the world and the crows were praying for, but it was major progress to me. Having taken those few steps, I knew I could press on, applying the determination that I had needed to succeed in sport, the single-mindedness of the wanderer and the presence of the Holy Spirit. I had entered another phase on the road to recovery.

Around this time, the BBC TV were interviewing young people on the road to recovery for their BBC Two Open Doors Programme. I was invited by producer Eddie Montague to take part in their filming schedule on 29th and 30th August 1979 for - 'Things Ain't What They Used To Be!' It was a rare break from the physical effort of rehabilitation and an opportunity for my ego to perk up again.

Prior to the BBC debut, I crossed another milestone. After fourteen weeks of disabled living, on August Bank Holiday, I embarked on my first sleepover at my own home in Wakefield. Mum and Dad were there to fuss and fluster around me, sleeping upstairs while I camped downstairs in the lounge. Still wheelchair and parent-dependent, but I was on the road to independent living. Mum and son were able to speak privately about her anguish and the irony of her wee boy being paralysed.

Mum 'laid on hands' and stood praying over me for four hours that afternoon, a significant time of breaking down barriers between mum and son and warfare in the spiritual realm, too.

In contrast to that personal milestone, in Ulster, the Provisional IRA captured the headlines. History would record the August Bank Holiday as the deadliest attack on the Army during the Troubles. A convoy was ambushed near Warrenpoint, killing eighteen soldiers at the foot of the beautiful Mourne Mountains. Later that day, on 27th August 1979, news broke that the Queen's cousin, Lord Mountbatten, had been assassinated with three others in Co. Sligo. These snippets of news brought a stark reminder of the world beyond my personal crisis. A world I was gradually returning to.

Through prayer networks and friends and family, my story was being told with varying degrees of accuracy. I was affronted by glib and, oft-times heartless, prosperity gospel-inspired 'name-it and claim-it' promises of physical healing. Spiritual things were being said from a position of medical ignorance, and many of the stories seemed to deny the fact that miracles were taking place on a daily basis. I had survived, and against the odds, I was learning to walk as a paraplegic, and when all around me felt like sinking sand, my limbs, my job, my possessions, I stood on solid ground, which was rock steady – Jesus.

Despite my reservations about dodgy spirituality, I began to receive invitations to speak at Churches, FGBUK, Charity events and Student Unions. Bretton College was the first place I spoke in public about my accident, and my diary hinted that a future in preaching might await:

> I went into the Spinal Injuries Unit gym early; the walking was easy. I wish every start could be as pain-free and spasm-free as today. I felt quite prayerful during the day, probably because I knew I could make a mess of the Bretton College meeting tonight. John Staley picked me up and took me to his place for tea.
>
> The rain poured down, plus thunder and lightning on the way to the college. We prayed as we went along in the car. It was a really nice atmosphere at Bretton, over 150 students there, singing their heads off in worship and a good deal of messing about as well – I enjoyed it. I gave my testimony, and the Lord helped me.
>
> Afterwards, I had a good chat with John about speaking in public for the Lord – Interesting!
>
> —Monday 3rd December 1979

Months went by; the walking improved, and stamina strengthened. Physiotherapist Roger became 'human,' Ron 'bald eagle' Mullins became a friend, and I began to take more trips outside the ward. Richard Shepley, a faithful friend, frequently ferried me from Hospital to Home, to church, restaurants, friends' houses, to work offices and to the airport for my first flight to Northern Ireland for Christmas with my family six months after the accident. I was not yet ready for a discharge from Pinderfields, but it was preparation for the resumption of normal daily life. These encounters beyond the ward as a disabled man helped me cope with the public's gawp and taught me, with the help of God, to balance humility and pride with dignity.

After eight exhausting, eventful months, I was finally discharged from the Spinal Injuries Unit on 28th January 1980. There was life after Honister.

EIGHT

Learning to Live Again

During my enforced time out from 'normal' everyday life in 1979, the world, surprisingly, continued to operate without me. In my absence, the United Kingdom managed to elect our first female Prime Minister, the Iron Lady, Margaret Thatcher. We were mutually oblivious to each other's new challenges. Likewise, in Cumbria, the town of Dalston, a few miles north of Honister, a sixth-form pupil was also unaware of my short stay in her neighbourhood in West Cumberland Hospital. In a parallel life story, Jennifer Downie was applying to study Music at Huddersfield University in Yorkshire. Neither of us knew that God's will and His perfect timing would bring us together.

Institutionalisation is a real danger for anyone who has had a long spell in hospital. After an eight-month stay, I had grown accustomed to the constant care, the camaraderie of staff and patients on the ward and the morning routine of rehab and friends visiting in afternoons and evenings. I needed to be weaned off Pinderfield's institutional care. If 1979 was learning to walk again, 1980 was learning to live again. I was apprehensive about this social rehabilitation and prayed for courage to adapt to life as a twenty-three-year-old rookie disabled bachelor. The spiritual reassurance and answers to my prayers came from the pages of the Holy Bible.

> Spoke to Dr Mulroy and he suggested that I should finally be discharged (after eight months of hospitalisation). I Went into Pinderfields Ward F1 gym for the last time. I feel the time is right for me to leave. I no longer belong here in hospital and to make the break now will be good for me. Bert and Pauline Sture (Bradford FGBUK president) came and took me home, and we had a good time of prayer and fellowship before they left. Our God reigns!
>
> —Wednesday 23rd January 1980
>
> Isaiah 12:2 spoke to me, 'Surely God is my salvation; I will trust and will not be afraid, for the Lord God is my strength and my might.'
>
> —Monday 4th February 1980
>
> Isaiah 26:3 spoke to me, 'You will keep in perfect peace him whose mind is steadfast, because he trusts in You…the Lord is the Rock eternal.'
>
> —Wednesday 6th February 1980
>
> Isaiah 28:16 spoke to me, 'This is what the Sovereign Lord says; 'See I lay a stone in Zion, a tested stone, a precious cornerstone for a sure foundation; the one who trusts will never be dismayed.'
>
> —Thursday 7th February 1980

My Wednesday bible reading (13th February) felt like a personal word about trusting God, an answer to my prayer about leaving the hospital. Any uncertainty and insecurity I felt at this time of transition melted away under the power of the word of God speaking directly to me. I could never believe that the Bible was just myth or history, prophecy, poetry or prose literature within two Testaments. This was the 'living word' in action; it seemed like some verses were in bolder typeface than the rest as my tutor, the Holy Spirit, taught that He knew the adversity I was going through and reassured me that He was with me and would lead me through it. The message seemed to be that I was entering a phase of quietness, trust and waiting on Him, learning to walk in his way (wherever that may be or whatever that may lead to).

> [15]In quietness and in trust shall be your strength...[18] 'blessed are all who wait for him'...[20] 'though the Lord gave you the bread of adversity and the water of affliction yet your Teacher will not hide himself anymore, but you will see your Teacher...[21]and your ears will hear a word behind you saying 'this is the way, walk in it'. (Isaiah 30)

The invitations to speak at Christian and non-Christian meetings began to trickle in, but my interpretation of the message from the Lord about 'quietness' was to turn down most of the openings and resume my accountancy studies.

Resuming work for Neville Russell (now Mazars) was more of a physical ordeal than I expected. The long layoff in Pinderfields Hospital had weakened me physically, and my decision to refuse the aid of a wheelchair for work and depend entirely on orthotic callipers and crutches was a bit foolhardy and seemed crazy to my work colleagues. Most lunch breaks were spent snoozing on the floor among clients' books in the walk-in cupboard. Once, one of the secretaries startled me with a scream. She entered the cupboard in darkness to retrieve some records, and there I was, laid flat out on the deck. She thought I had collapsed, gave a yell, and ran out of the cupboard to fetch the first aiders! I gave up the midday closet kip after that!

The stamina returned slowly, as did the desire to study for my final Accountancy exam. When an opportunity arose to attend a residential course, I snapped up the firm's generous offer to cover the costs. The year began in residency at Pinderfields Hospital and concluded with a residency at the Old Park Hotel for a two-month block of study leave at the Accountancy Tuition Centre in St Lawrence on the Isle of Wight. It was my first trip to the Island whose beauty had influenced literary greats: Dickens, Tennyson, Lewis Carroll, Rudyard Kipling and JB Priestly. It was the tonic I needed; the course was intense, but it led me by the scruff of the neck back into study mode. I totally fell in love with the Isle of Wight.

At the end of a hard day's slog, while fellow students relaxed in the hotel bar, I preferred to unwind at Ventnor seafront and hop on my crutches along the esplanade as the waves lapped over the golden sands below. I was finding my feet in many ways. The incessant pounding of the sea waves on the sandy beach with the backdrop of St Boniface Downs was a peaceful oasis after a traumatic year. Along Undercliff Drive, Ventnor Botanic Gardens was another refreshing retreat into quiet times with my Lord Jesus. These were revitalising encounters with the author of this beautiful creation. As the Island's motto puts it so aptly, 'All this beauty is of God!'

Each Sunday, I took a Sabbath rest, which meant personal time off accountancy tuition. The first church I came across was a modest Free Evangelical Church on Alpine Road, Ventnor. Grey heads on charcoal grey suit jackets turned to observe the clatter of a newcomer arriving on crutches. A family of five occupied the back row, and hop-a-long slid alongside them. It was a typical 'Old Time Religion' service where an elder 'brought a word' to the congregation after a number of Moody and Sankey hymns and extempore prayers from whoever felt led to intercede.

The welcome extended after that gospel meeting was another tonic to my soul. There I was, three hundred miles from home, in the company of strangers who quickly became family, Christian brothers and sisters. The Wells family invited me back for Sunday lunch, which extended to tea and concluded with a guest appearance at the Youth Club that was held in their home. It felt like home from home, family from family, and I scrounged many a coffee from John and Margie Wells over the ten study weeks that followed. This would turn out to be a significant friendship, instrumental to my recovery and formative in future decisions about Accountancy and Christian ministry.

The Chartered Accountant's certificate that adorned the office wall was the positive outcome of the Island studies. But there was something else going on: that Alpine Road youth group planted a seed in my heart for youth work. After returning home to Wakefield, I accepted an invitation to lead St Andrew's Church youth club with Architect Richard Shepley. There was, however, a slight problem; the youth club met in a small flat on the third floor of the vicarage!

On my first evening in charge of the club, I stood at the foot of the three flights and said to a few youths, 'What do we do now?'

'We'll get Big Neil!'

A stampede of feet trotted up the stairway and returned promptly with Big Neil Kellett. Neil had just been offered a professional contract with Castleford Rugby Football Club as a front-row prop. He stood tall, square and broad, like a six-foot cube.

'All reet cock!' Neil greeted his new youth leader.

'Gi'e these bairns thy crutches, and A'll carry thee oop theeer.'

In an instant, the Lord gave me the wisdom not to argue and just do what he says. It's best to obey Big Neil. The Rugby Prop then tackled me in the groin region and draped me over his shoulder like a limp roll of carpet. The three bumpy flights of stairs happened in a flash; the Rugby League professional dealt with me like a training ground exercise.

For the disabled Irishman, it was a good initiation into the leadership of the youth club in the heart of Wakefield's notorious Eastmoor Estate.

In subsequent weeks, we developed a system that would traumatise any Health and Safety officer. I would arrive at the foot of the stairs, and a plastic garden chair would appear. I was relieved of my crutches and seated on the chair, then two youths would haul me up the three flights to the 'youth suite.' It was a promising start to my youth work career, a fine icebreaker at the beginning of each meeting, a good witness to Christ's sustaining power and a lesson in humility for me. It was a ministry that would last over ten years.

The Honister accident had rocked the people at St Andrew's Church. I was one of twenty young people from this church enjoying a week away together in the Lake District when tragedy struck. People had been praying for us on this trip, praying for safety. Now they were asking what had happened to all those prayers; were they ignored, unheard, ineffective? The 'why' question lurked behind each thought and conversation. It's a question I had faced myself many times. Usually, my response was, 'Why not?' As Christians, we are not cocooned from accidents and illnesses. The Bible says in John 16:33, 'In this world you will have trouble. But take heart! I [Jesus] have overcome the world.' The voice of the Lord that I heard on Honister Cragg said, 'I am with you always' (Matthew 28:20). That was the promise I received then, and my subsequent experience of God speaking through bible verses has been a special time of close intimacy with my heavenly Father. Gradually, I gained confidence in speaking out at church about this assurance.

I learnt to leave the 'Why me' question hanging, preferring to use a 'Help me' prayer instead.

Besides, there was a lot of good stuff going on around me at St Andrew's; people flourished in trying to support me.

Some offered helping hands, and others boldly gave me scripture verses to encourage me. Perhaps this flourishing was a partial answer to the 'why' question. I preferred to see this acute time of loving Christian fellowship as proof that our Lord can turn any crisis into a victory for those who turn to Him with the 'help me' prayer.

Many of my neighbours also adopted me as extended family after I returned home. Roger and a bunch of local men drew me into their acoustic folk group, and I enjoyed making a joyful noise with those guys. They were very much a part of my restorative healing. A Christian couple, Phil and Wendy, included me in their family's Sunday meal after church every week for several years.

'We aren't going to ask you every week, but we do expect you to tell us if you are not coming!' said Wendy after church.

Thus, I became part of the Bootles - enjoying the status of adopted older brother to Jane, Matt and Helen. Some neighbours randomly brought meals to my door while others mowed the lawn. The youth club tended the garden a few times, planting random shrubs and perennials in the middle of the lawn. I'm not sure their future was in garden design! Nonetheless, I was privileged to be a catalyst of many acts of human kindness and generosity.

My obsessive drive for independent living had to give way to the outflow of love around me. It was a truly humbling experience. I had spent most of my life, to this point, playing the part of the loner, the wanderer, the self-sufficient one. My year in rehab taught me to walk again. Now, I was being educated in receiving, in being served by others, in being needy and vulnerable. It was a difficult lesson for a rover but a precious one: food for my soul. My teacher, the Holy Spirit, showed me, again from the Bible, that it was a hard lesson for Saint Peter, too. In John 13, when Jesus draped a flannel over his arm and offered to wash Peter's feet, Pete said, 'No way, Lord, you can't serve me.'

But Jesus was teaching him another lesson, not about serving but about learning to be served, the humility and vulnerability of receiving from others. Like Peter, I began to realise the privilege and beauty of this low place and prayed in Aramaic, 'Bring it on, Lord.'

My beloved Ford Capri was fitted with hand controls, meaning I no longer had to rely on friends taxiing me to places. Longer trips driving back to Northern Ireland, up to Scotch Corner and across the A66 to Carlisle and on to Stranraer, crossing by Ferry to Larne, built up my confidence that I could travel independently. My mother had ministered many times in Oklahoma, and I had an open invitation to stay in Tulsa with the McNutt's and to visit the Oral Roberts University campus. Mum had been invited by Oral Roberts to the inauguration of the University in 1966, and I wanted to see and experience the original 24/7 prayer tower.

Richard Shepley accompanied me on my first excursion to the USA as a young disabled man. I chose to travel without a wheelchair, preferring yet again crutches and orthotic calliper propulsion. I didn't budget for the vast distances from check-in to departure gate, and I confess I was exhausted before I even got to the Transatlantic aeroplane. It would have been sensible to include a wheelchair in my baggage. I was too pig-headed to admit it.

Max McNutt met me in Tulsa, Oklahoma, while Richard flew on to Texas. We drove to the Oral Roberts University Campus and visited the magnificent 200-foot prayer tower with its 360° hub observation deck that maintained a 24/7 prayer vigil. On 30th May 1979, they had been part of a global network of intercession for my survival and ultimate healing.

Richard and I met up again in Los Angeles for the final leg of our USA trip. We stayed in Hacienda Heights, Los Angeles, with Giff Claiborne and family. Giff was a senior pastor at Faith Community Church with Pastor Jim Reeve. Rita Burke met Giff while ministering in the States in 1970.

He was interested in how I reacted to my mother's healing ministry following the accident and life-changing disability. I had received many prolonged times of prayer for healing from Rita. The reality remained that I was still paralysed. I could see the truth that I had experienced many healings to survive thus far. However, the massive life change following such trauma did not significantly affect me as an accountant. Fortunately, I could still earn a living from this profession. I still held the view that I would remain a bachelor throughout my life, but I was not going to let the accident or disability define me.

Towards the end of our stay, Giff prayed with me, 'laying on hands' as Jesus did in Luke 4:40 and the early Christians did in Acts 8:17. During this prayer time, Giff stopped abruptly, looked me in the eye, and said prophetically, 'sometime in the future you are going to be involved in the healing ministry, not exactly like your mother but the healing ministry nonetheless.'

Astonished, I replied, 'I'm the world's worst advert for the healing ministry, the best example of unanswered prayer. What confidence would people have if the person praying for them was broken himself?'

He smiled wryly and said, 'That's God's problem; God will use your brokenness to minister to others; there will be implicit empathy.'

I quietened my protestations, and we resumed our prayer time.

After a period of quiet solitude, Giff spoke again, a stern word, about relationships. 'Kelvin, the Lord has a partner for you.' Using the words of Genesis 2:18, he said, 'It is not good for the man to be alone.' Kelvin, do not resist the blessing that the Lord has in store for you.'

I mulled these prophetic words over in my mind as we flew back to Manchester Airport. Like other words of promise or prophecy, I shelved them, not knowing what else to do with them. In the meantime, I carried on with my accountancy work.

In the years that followed, St Andrew's attracted a healthy group of young Christians. Many of the church youth club attended the Sunday evening services at St Andrew's. They commandeered the rear left nave of the church, and I sat amongst them. There was the usual conflict of holy and unholy banter as testosterone-charged youths flirted with Anglican liturgy and the opposite sex in equal measure. Some of the older lads took an interest in the students from the local Bretton College. They travelled to St Andrew's evening service because it was known as an 'evangelical church.'

Teen Dave nudged me during the last verse of 'Shine Jesus Shine,'

'Do you see that pretty brunette in the purple Rah-rah skirt?'

'Shush, Dave, she's too old for you.'

'I bet I can get off with her,' Dave crowed as we sat down for intercessions. I foolishly retorted. 'Behave, Dave, there's more chance of me getting off with her.'

Eighteen-year-old Dave pushed his chest out like a banty-cock and challenged me, 'Bet you a fiver, I get off with her first!'

'Sit still and massage your eyebrows, Dave; we're supposed to be praying.'

It's hard to believe that God was interested in our conversation simultaneously as the rest of our congregation was interceding for world peace. Just another typical exchange between youth leader and youth and part of the road to recovery for the wanderer whose wings had been clipped. Mysteriously, God was engineering a testosterone-charged encounter.

In the parallel life, the young Rah-rah student had come to Bretton College for her Teachers Training PGCE year, having graduated in Music from Huddersfield University. Yorkshire seemed a long, lonely way from her home and family in Dalston, Cumbria. Her letter to Bryan Ellis, the vicar of St Andrew's, asked if a Christian family would rent a room to her for her ten-month course at Bretton.

Jennifer Downie had become a Christian in her penultimate

year at Huddersfield and wanted to be included in a Christian family rather than face the solitude of Halls of Residence at Bretton. The College was set in the artistic splendour of the Yorkshire Sculpture Park. Sheep grazing on undulating hills, balancing lakes, and Sir Henry Moore sculptures surrounded the stately home and halls at the centre of the College. But for a newly born-again Christian, it was a college campus ten miles from the nearest town and a student ghetto away from the hustle and bustle of everyday life.

'Who's the man with the artificial legs?' Jennifer asked Anita, her host.

'That's Kelvin, he's the youth leader. He's an eligible bachelor, but he has a bit of a reputation as a flirt. You don't want to get involved there.'

Jennie had just ended a long-standing relationship with her non-Christian boyfriend in Dalston and had no intention of getting involved with anyone for a while. She was on her final teaching practice and had secured her first teaching position at Joseph Rowntree School in York. After eight months of PGCE study, Jennie was looking forward to summer with her family in the Lake District and a new life in historic York.

Greg and Anita were my co-workers in the church youth club, and one evening, I called around to devise our Summer Youth programme. The planning meeting included a meal, and our waitress for the evening was Rah-rah Jennie. For starters, she placed a bowl of cold pea soup with a dollop of cream in front of me.

'Waitress, this soup's cold.' I complained.

'It's consommé, actually, sir.'

There was chemistry between us from the first to the last

course. When our waitress sat down to join us for the main course, my heart skipped a beat. I was bowled over by more than the cold soup. I was determined to keep any whiff of interest in the lodger from Anita. Consequently, I hardly spoke to Jennie throughout the meal. I was so intensely focused on youth club business that I was even boring myself. But there were glances and half smiles and, at one point, a deliberately accidental touch of hands. Something started that night, and my Ford Capri drove itself home on autopilot. I went to sleep wondering if I could pluck up the courage to ask her on a date. What would she think of dating a disabled man? Could I face the possibility of rejection from a pretty young Bretton student? Was this all a big fantasy in my head? Was God in this, or was it just a flirtation? Questions ricocheted around my mind as I drifted off to sleep.

I remembered Giff Claiborne's prophetic word in my morning 'quiet time.' As I prepared spiritually for the working day, my thoughts were hijacked by prayers about this new girl who had captivated my thoughts overnight. 'Lord, I want to stay in the centre of your will; if this is all wrong, make something happen that will quell my thoughts and shut down my feelings for Jennie.'

I clock-watched till 5.15 pm and dashed home from work; I was going to ask her out. I picked up the phone and paused.... what would I do if Anita picked up the phone, 'Lord, make Jennie pick up the phone as a sign that you are in this', I prayed. I felt like a novice highboard diver looking over the edge of the 27-metre platform.

After a dozen rings, a young female answered the phone,

'Is that Jennie?'

'Yes, is that Kelvin?'

'How did you know it was me?'

'There's not many people with Irish accents who phone this number. I'm afraid neither Greg nor Anita are in. Would you like me to take a message?'

'No, it's you I want, err sorry, I didn't mean to say that, it's you I wanted to speak to, err, have you got a minute to talk.'

'Yes, carry on, what do you want?'

'I wondered if you'd like to go out on a kind of datie restaurantie chatty thingy to get to know you.'

'I think you're asking me out, is that right?'

'That's a bit simpler than I put it, but yes, can we?'

'Kelvin, do you know I leave Wakefield in two weeks?'

'Two weeks!'

'I've finished my course; I'm going back to Dalston to see my family, and from there, I move to York for a teaching job after the summer.'

'Well, I guess we've got a fortnight then. Can we still go out?'

Jennie hesitated; the silence was agony.

'I suppose we can get to know each other.'

'Can we start tonight?'

'I'm sorry, I'm going out for a meal tonight at a friend's house.'

'I'll pick you up from there afterwards, and we'll go somewhere nice.'

'You don't waste any time, do you?'

'You told me I only had two weeks!'

And that was the arrangement finalised for the first date. I rolled the sunroof back on my Ford Capri, tied a bandana around my receding hairline and collected Jennie after the meal at her friend Rachel's.

We drove to Newmillerdam, one of Wakefield's popular beauty spots, and started the getting-to-know-you process.

'I've never been out with a Christian before', Jennie blurted.

'Well, it's not a lot different. We still like to kiss and cuddle, but Jesus is the centre of the relationship, so I'd like us to pray together.'

I was surprised by my own boldness, and Jennie seemed a bit taken aback by the abruptness or the idea of praying together (or both). But that's exactly how we started our first date. As we sat looking over the evening sunset silhouetting the purple blooming laurels reflecting on Newmillerdam's waters, we prayed briefly and simply that Christ would be in the centre of everything we said and did together. The kiss came later. That evening!

I coped well with the two-week time pressure. I visited her 'digs' at Greg and Anita's every day. They say the way to a man's heart is through his stomach, and my belly fell in love with Jennie's well-filled homemade sandwiches.

Being a newly qualified Chartered Accountant, I had just started a new job as a Company Accountant for William Sugden's, part of the Double Two Shirt Group and manufacturers of Jet Jeans and one of the leading suppliers of uniforms and workwear in the UK. I had just enough time in my lunch hour to nip out from Sugden's for a sandwich and a catch-up. The romance flourished over the fortnight. There were several evenings of walks, talks, prayer and laughter, and by the end of the second week, we had condensed the getting-to-know-you process. On the fourteenth day, I admitted that I was in love and that I wished to keep the courtship going despite the long distance from Wakefield to Dalston.

The two-hour weekend drive from Yorkshire to Cumbria's Lake District seemed a short hop. I was driving to see my new love, and the A66 across the Yorkshire Dales looking onwards to the peaks of the Lake District was enthralling. One of those peaks was Honister Cragg, but it was fast fading as a painful memory and rapidly becoming a new raison d'etre for me.

I was also moving on from something else that had been highly significant in my able-bodied life. While I was getting to know Jennie, in the summer of 1984, the Los Angeles Olympics were in full flow, and my heart was overjoyed to see my Wakefield Hockey captain, Norman Hughes, lead the British Men's Hockey team to a bronze medal, beating the Aussies 3 – 2 in the playoff for third place.

As Britain caught the hockey bug and Hughes, Sean Kerley, Ian Taylor, and Billy McConnell became household names, I prayed that the Lord would ease the disappointment of losing the opportunity to compete for a place in that team. I had first played with Billy McConnel for Northern Ireland schoolboys at Dublin's famous Lansdowne Road stadium in 1972; now, in 1984, his achievement brought bittersweet memories. His presence in the British team, standing on that bronze podium on 11th August 1984, seemed to emphasise my paralysis, and I sat alone at home in Wakefield watching the television with tears streaming down my cheeks. In a strange way, that day a burden was lifted from me: the healing of an unachievable goal through the thrill of their battling encounters, punching above their weight and my genuine joy for them. They were tears of pride and joy rather than pain and loss. It felt good to be free of that hurt, and I sensed God's whisper through the scriptures, 'Humble yourself, under God's mighty hand, that he may lift you up in due time. Cast all your cares on him because he cares for you.' 1 Peter 5:7.

I was due to meet Jennie's parents a week later, and as it turned out, it was not a straightforward affair! Alec and Joan Downie were caravanning at Dent by the River Dee with the iconic Ribblehead viaduct nearby. My heart sank as I drove onto the caravan site. I was to meet the parents in a caravan! A caravan which was totally inaccessible! I spotted the tiny, rickety, free-standing, open-fronted metal step into the narrow caravan doorway, which was two feet above ground level. On crutches and full-length rigid orthotic callipers on my legs, there was no way I could get into that caravan - it looked impossible. I wanted to pull a handbrake turn and speed home to Wakefield.

Jennie came to meet me as my broad shoulders heaved the metalled legs out of the car. Her Father, Alec Downie, came to the caravan door and greeted me;

'You must be Kelvin; I've heard a lot about you; come in, lad.'

'Err, I'm afraid I can't come in.'

'Why ever not? Don't be shy.'

'No, Mr Downie, shy is not something I do. I don't think I can get into your caravan!'

'Come on, I'll give you a hand.'

My first meeting with Alec Downie, a local preacher in the Methodist Church, was not the customary handshake.

I stretched my arm around his bony shoulders and barked, 'Stand still while I use your height to lift myself into the caravan.' Dignity was low on the agenda as I scrambled up the caravan's north face, landing against the melamine dining table opposite the doorway.

'Hello, Mrs Downie, that wasn't a very slick entrance.'

'Never mind, we're not very slick in our family, Kelvin; welcome to our humble abode.'

Alec Downie had tears in his eyes as he said, 'It's not right that bad things happen to good people; you have so much of your life ahead of you and,' he nodded at my legs, 'something like that happens.'

'Bad things happen to many people, Mr Downie and how we respond to these things is what shapes our character.'

'But you're a young Christian man; did you never question why?'

'Not really; I believe the Lord kept me alive for a reason, and I just hope I can glorify Him in the way I deal with this handicap.'

'I admire you son. Joan put the kettle on and give the lad a cup of tea.'

It was near midnight when Jen and I left the caravan site and drove to Dalston village for my first stop-over. The entrance to their family home was not straightforward either. It had a bit of deja vue of the caravan experience. This time, I had no bony shoulder to hoist me through the doorway.

It was a dark starlit night in Dalston, and mixed aromas hung heavy in the humid midnight air. Alec Downie had been tending his roses and dung vied with rose scent for prominence. My heart raced with butterflies as I faced the two awkward steps into their home.

Jennie went in ahead of me, unaware of my fears and the danger ahead. I lodged my crutches up one rung and took off, intending a perfect landing on the first step. The toes touched down nicely, but the heels caught on the lip, and I slowly toppled backwards rigidly. I stared up at the starry night sky as I lay in the pungent midnight manure-doused flowerbed.

By now, my dignity was shot to pieces as I entered The Forge, the Downie homestead, on my posterior with rose-dung stains on my trousers. Jennie came running as the stinking wanderer hauled himself up the two offending steps and over the threshold. I shuffled on my backside into the lounge and remained on the floor as she sat on the settee bewildered. I thought to myself, 'In for a penny, in for a pound,' and flipping myself onto both paralysed knees swaying gently, out of control, I held my sweetheart's hand (more for balance than affection) and said, 'Jennie I've been waiting for this moment all my life, now, here I am covered in manure, and I'm asking you - will you marry me, muck and all!'

'Well, I never expected a proposal in this way, but the answer is 'yes.'

It was probably the least romantic proposal of all times, but I did manage to wobble on bended knees before transferring up onto the settee where I slept for the night.

That was the easy bit: how was I going to tell Billy and Rita Burke, in Northern Ireland, that I was going to marry an English girl!

NINE

Lake of Tears

Alec Downie never expressed unease about his daughter marrying a paraplegic when I formally asked if I could have his blessing to marry Jennie. Nor did he seem concerned that a whirlwind five-week relationship resulted in a rapid engagement. The protocol trip to Northern Ireland held more trepidation. Would the Burke's welcome an English lass into the family with the likelihood that our married future could lie beyond the Emerald Isle? There was still an understanding that 'wee Kelvin' would come back and 'do the accounts for Burkes of Cornascriebe', especially now that Mr Spencer, their accountant, had retired.

Perhaps it wasn't Jennie's best decision to dye her hair black with broad crimson streaks. And there's more; stripy dungarees may have been in fashion in Yorkshire, but they were out of place in Portadown, where Christian ladies were wearing appropriate blouses and dress skirts with scarf accessories held together with modest broach. Unperturbed, that is how Jennie turned out for 'meeting the in-laws.' Foolishly, I told her she looked like 'a sack of potatoes', which didn't put her in the best of moods for her 'Burke encounter.'

Bizarrely, as my mum Rita formally shook Jennie's hand, she said she 'had a dream last night' that 'Kelvin's girl had red and black hair.' We took that as a word from the Lord and moved on into the kitchen and sat round the old mahogany table that has been in the family for as long as I could remember.

The tension around the table was palpable as we shared a meal together.

Jennie said it was more like an interview than a conversation! My Father's friend, Jim, had been invited to join us for the meal, and his brief seemed to be to discern if Jennie 'was after my money!' He was alarmed to hear that the only collateral Jennie brought to the partnership was a car loan and an upright satin mahogany Chappell piano.

George Allen, another of Father's advisors, arrived later, and we sat in the lounge in our family home. George, as he usually did, produced his little notebook and brought a 'word' from the Lord. Proverbs 3:5-6: 'Trust in the Lord with all your heart and lean not on your own understanding; in all your ways acknowledge him, and he will direct your paths.'

We felt reassured as Uncle George said in his 'wee word,'

'Well, Kelvie, I think you've found a great wee lassie.

One who loves you, and I can see that you love her. The two of you are about to get into the wheelbarrow together, and the Lord is at the handles. Trust him, and he will direct you. Not just your marriage, your jobs, your health, your family - your whole lives.'

He went on, 'A hundred years ago, a man walked across the Niagara Falls on a tightrope, then he took a sack of potatoes across the falls in a wheelbarrow. He asked someone on the

Falls if he believed he could carry a person across the falls, and the person said he did. But when Blondin invited him to get in the barrow, he wouldn't trust the high-wire artist.

The pair of you are getting into the wheelbarrow, and you just need to trust the one who is at the handles – He will direct your paths!'

The following day, I had to take Jennie to see Auntie Florence at Ballynagarrick. Florence would give an opinion on behalf of the McMurray side of the family (mothers), and we got through that audition as well.

We laughed afterwards about the interrogation, and it would appear that Jennie passed the Jim Wilson test. In truth, both of our parents were more relieved that our relationship was 'centred' on God. Just as we prayed together on our first date, we continued that practice of praying together when we met up, often sharing a reading from the Bible and learning from each other. It has been a rule of life that has continued to sustain us through life's journey.

After the rapid engagement, we applied the brakes and courted for two years while Jennie taught Music at Joseph Rowntree Grammar School in York before moving back to a teaching post in the music department at Ossett High School in Wakefield.

Our wedding day at St. Andrew's Church, Wakefield, on 2nd August 1986, was a special wedding in many ways. The Best Men, Richard Shepley, my travelling companion, and my brother Richard, reluctantly wore my chosen wedding attire. Suited in silver grey Burton suits and peach bow ties, we looked more like the Commodores about to go on stage than a groom and best men!

Jennie and I had caused an upset by choosing to get married in St Andrew's, the church where we first met, where I was a youth leader and where the local Christian family had been so supportive throughout my Spinal Injury recovery and our engagement. We expected a boycott by relatives, but there was an overwhelmingly positive response from our travelling friends and relations from as far away as Australia and greater numbers from Northern Ireland and the English Lake District.

My Ulster travellers amused my Wakefield neighbours over the days leading up to the wedding. It appeared that if you can't bring the bride and groom to Ireland, then Ireland would come to Yorkshire. The Irish custom of 'sweeping the yard' before the groom leaves the paternal home for the last time was invoked on the homestead in Sandal. Yard brushes dutifully swept the drives of the neighbourhood. Wild horses couldn't pull my Aunty Eddie away from the yard as they brushed around the modern housing estate on the wedding morn before we set off to St Andrew's Church.

I shunned the offer of a wheelchair throughout the ceremony, and after the marriage, I hopped down the church aisle on crutches with Jennie on my arm, feeling that the trauma of the past seven years was ebbing away. I continued to eschew the idea that mobility would be faster and easier in a wheelchair, preferring the Hop-along Cassidy look.

As a result, I developed a Charles Atlas top, and Max Wall bottom look as my shoulders took on the chores the bottom half refused to do.

Jennie and I started our new life together in my two-story 'Bachelor pad' in Wakefield. My determination to return to live in that home and climb the flight of stairs several times daily was met with muted resistance by my wife.

For me, it was important to set and achieve these personal goals, to redeem inaccessible areas that were expected to be lost because of the disability. I felt like I was on a personal mission to refuse this disability the attention it craved. I personified the paralysis as the enemy within, which helped me press on despite the handicap.

After a decade, there was still a mood of optimism that this accident would be a beacon of God's healing power. My mother, Rita, was still active in speaking at Christian conferences and in the healing ministry. She was convinced that there would be a miraculous outcome to this tragedy. In addition, Christian friends and family continued to send cards and letters with prophecies of physical healing and bible verses with healing promises, such as 1 Peter 2:24, 'by Christ's stripes you are healed.'

Molly, one of St Andrew's quieter, unassuming members, woke one night from her sleep in February 1990 having had a dream of a promise that I would be healed before the end of July 1990. She approached our new minister, Rev John Ross, who confirmed that there were several other 'words of knowledge' that confirmed this promise.

I recorded in my diary on 30th May 1990

> It seems appropriate to record on the 11th anniversary of my accident that several words of knowledge have been given that I will be healed in July. I am committed to this healing; I desire it with all my heart and will attempt to stand on the word which has been given.
>
> I have asked the Lord to confirm the word and then I received a phone call from Mum last week that an American preacher had prophesied that she would have the desire of her heart in July. I believe I will receive this healing this summer and from now on

negative thoughts or doubts will be rebuked (James 1:6). Jesus is the healer; if he has decreed that I will be healed, then I will be healed.

Rev John Ross and a small team of devoted intercessors, Kevin, Gareth, Molly and my wife Jennie, met weekly at his vicarage to lay on hands and pray in faith, believing that this 'word' would be fulfilled. In reality, I struggled with being the constant focus of their intercessions, but I desperately sought the promised healing and wrestled and rebuked any negativity in case my scepticism would thwart the Holy Spirit's healing powers.

Three days before the healing deadline, we met to pray. There was an air of expectation that we had not experienced before. I wondered if this was the 'gift of faith' mentioned in the first letter to the Corinthians (Chapter 12). During prayers and prayerful silence, Gareth said he had a picture of a severed spinal cord that had moved to within a hair's breadth of joining. Rev Ross encouraged us to pray fearlessly for that final connection that would result in physical healing. All in all, we prayed for two solid hours and at the end of the session, the pastor said he believed the time was right to speak directly to me, as Jesus spoke to the paralysed man in the Gospel of Mark 2:11 'get up and walk.'

I assured him that I was ready to step out believing the word. I reminded the group that the nature of paralysis meant that I could not even move one muscle to start the process; apart from my own expectancy and confidence, that 'step' would have to be the supernatural work of the Holy Spirit.

We were all on the edge of our seats, literally. Gareth and John took hold of my two arms, and I said at the right time, 'Help me out of the chair, and I will yearn with all my heart and mind to receive healing.'

The Reverend commanded, 'In the name of Jesus, rise up and walk!'

At that point, I launched myself upwards with every fibre of my body. For a brief moment, I thought, 'I'm up; it has worked; I'm healed,' I sensed that I was standing on my own legs with two helpers on each shoulder. Just as rapidly, my elation subsided as I crumpled beneath paralysed legs. The men tried to hold me aloft like a powerless marionette, but it was clear for all to see that I was still paralysed. I softly asked the two aides to lower me back down.

Undeterred, I was encouraged and spoke positively about the experience. I was buoyed by the momentary feeling of healing success, and at the end of the evening, we vowed to keep praying as the original word was that the miracle would take place before the end of July. There were still three days to go.

On the 29th July 1990, I wrote:

> My thoughts are constantly on my healing. After praying with [Rev]John and Gareth last Saturday, I said to the Lord, 'I am walking away from my wheelchair, away from my callipers, away from my disability.' Gareth has been given a picture of 'a hairline crack in a cup' and believes it is a picture of all that is separating my spinal cord from being re-joined. I feel my faith is increasing; John and Gareth felt it may have been possible to be healed yesterday but probably tomorrow.

I knew that if this miracle were to occur, it would be newsworthy and in daydreams, I held imaginary chat show conversations with chat show hosts Terry Wogan and Michael Parkinson about the way this miracle developed and how it was undeniable proof of the existence of God who sought a personal relationship with us and was responsive to the 'prayer of faith.' Secretly, I had even gone into the woods at Newmillerdam with a camcorder to record on VHS-C what I expected to be 'before and after' shots of my mode of walking before the miracle with the discarded crutches and calliper-free dance to be added after 31st July.

Supernatural healing and the 'prayer of faith' were also prevalent in the wider Christian church at this time. It was an intense time of miraculous expectations of the 'signs and wonders' variety as championed by John Wimber and Anglicised by Rev. David Watson, the minister at St Michael le Belfrey in York. I attended many healing conferences and often found myself in the middle of a prayer scrum where I was the 'oval ball' in the middle of hopeful budding amateur intercessors reaching out healing hands to the needy invalid.

Invariably, I felt pressure to fulfil their expectations and lamely 'leap for joy.'

Unfortunately, there was nothing short of a heaven-sent miracle that would enable me to perform such a wonder.

Being paralysed meant I couldn't even take a physical step of faith! I found myself spiralling into despair that I was letting the Christian world down by continuing to remain unhealed and disabled.

John Wimber, at a local conference in Normanton, Yorkshire, spoke compassionately to me, 'The weight of healing expectation is a burden you do not have to bear. Your feeling of failure is not a prompting of the Holy Spirit. I apologise for my prayer team who have given you the impression that your healing is being withheld because of something you are failing to do.'

Wimber laid his hand on my head and urged 'more [Holy Spirit] power' to fuse severed spinal cord nerve ends. I experienced a glow of Holy Spirit fire flowing through the

Wimber conduit. It was a special moment, but at the end of the conference, I still required the hand controls on my Ford Capri to drive home to Wakefield. I sat up till midnight talking with Jennie about how people in the healing ministry, after their healing meetings, return to their homes, switch off their bedside light for the night in their everyday able-bodied life with no concept of the hurt that 'unsuccessful' prayer ministry might have caused to the 'needy' who return home still nursing their needs.

It felt like I was in a spiritual battle where I was the battleground. God seemed impersonal, but I yearned with all my heart for a personal touch. I wouldn't admit it, but, in truth, I began to wallow in the mire of self-pity. Outwardly, I was the same crazy extrovert Irishman who was coping well, declaring in faith that I believed the Lord would heal me, that I would be a testimony to the one true, living God active in a world of false gods of sport, fast cars and celebrities. However, the public saw a different view to that of the inner self.

The intercessors' team prayed faithfully for the last time on 31st July 1990. It was an evening of positive sound bites and declarations of faith; 'It's nearly there,' 'Reach out and receive it,' 'Take the Lord's hand and step out of the wheelchair.'

Expectancy was soaring, and at the repeat of the pastor's 'rise up and walk in the name of Jesus' command, I gave a mental instruction for these paralysed legs to straighten, lock, rise up and step out. Alas, the paralysis prevented any of the afore, not even as much as a twitch of a limb. The Holy Spirit-charged prayer meeting lasted four hours until I reminded the group after midnight that July had passed. Molly's prophecy was unfulfilled as 31st July 1990 slipped into August.

In the following days, I was overcome with sadness. I could

not even record my disappointment in my diary; a blank entry said it all. I declined the Rev Ross's intercessors' invitation to continue to meet and pray. The conversations after the deadline passed seemed to imply that I had allowed negativity to enter and deny me the miracle I so hoped for. The implication was that God was dangling a healing in front of me like a carrot before a pleasure-beach donkey. It was, oh so close to me and if I reached out for that miracle in the correct way and exuded sufficient faith and rebuked all doubt and ensured no malice or ill feeling was directed towards the driver of the car, then, and only then would Almighty God grant the healing.

I was confused, deflated and unable to share my pain and devastation with anyone, not even Jennie. This did not sound like my Abba Father, my loving heavenly Father who had my name engraved on the palm of his hands (Isaiah 49:16).

I reflected that the Lord Jesus never presented hurdles to be vaulted before he declared his healings; his spoken word, 'rise up and walk,' was the same creative force as at the birth of time. I became more and more convinced that this 'carrot-dangling' God was not a scriptural portrayal of the one true God, but I did not know how to deal with the deep sadness that I felt. The prayer group wanted to support me, but I didn't need comforting, I didn't need explanations, the reality was brutal enough – I wasn't physically healed.

A few months later, internationally renowned authority in the healing ministry, Francis MacNutt, came to Wakefield to speak. I telephoned my mother in Ireland as I knew she had often spoken of meeting and ministering with Francis MacNutt in the 1970s. Mum's approach to the healing ministry could be described as prolonged prayer, and MacNutt also endorsed that patient perseverance in prayer for healing, which was quite time-consuming and unspectacular, but diligent and devoted to waiting on the Lord Jesus and seeking a gradual divine healing for the seeker.

Thus, encouraged by Rita to attend, I found myself on the front pew in Wakefield Cathedral listening to a powerful sermon delivered gently by soft-spoken ex-Dominican Priest MacNutt about his experiences of the effectiveness of continuing prayer or 'soaking prayer' over a longer time period. I believed I had been engaging in this depth of prayer for healing with Rev Ross' group over several months, so I was hopeful that prayer ministry at the laying on of hands of Francis MacNutt would reap benefits of some sort.

As MacNutt concluded his talk, he asked if 'some people have come here this evening needing a physical healing miracle. I tentatively raised my hand and glanced over my shoulder. To my amazement, approximately one-third of the congregation had hands raised. He then invited any who would like prayer ministry to come to the front. Despite the fact that I was seated on the front pew, by the time I got my orthotic locked and crutches at the ready, I was already three rows back in the pecking order from a MacNutt moment.

We waited patiently for a 'touch' while the music group played Fisherfolk and Harvesttime classics. Three-quarters of an hour later, I was still stood waiting and my legs were beginning to shake rapidly in a spasm from standing too long in the callipers. A voice over the microphone said there were too many for MacNutt to see, and counsellors would come and minister to those who were still to be prayed for.

Maureen was my counsellor, and she was most impressed by the way the Holy Spirit was shaking me from foot to head. We said 'Hi' to each other, and I assured her the shake was actually muscle spasm.

'Oh, I don't know,' she said, 'the Spirit can surprise us in that way.'

'Yes, I know, but this is definitely spasm.'

She continued her line of inquiry, asking about my legs and asked me about the car crash. I tried to keep my replies as brief as possible as I had already decided to make a beeline for the back door.

Maureen's detective work led her to suggest to me that the reason why I was still not healed after so many years was due to a grudge that I was holding against someone. Ludicrous, I thought, you know nothing about me, and that's how you feel led by the Lord to counsel me! The only grudge I was holding was against Maureen with her amateur psychotherapy.

Actually, I wasn't angry, I could see the funny side of it. I had come to sit at the feet of MacNutt, who my mother knows, and I can't get near him. Instead, I get Maureen! In the end, I made an excuse that I couldn't stand the spasm any longer. Maureen replied, 'I just feel the Lord is telling me to give you a big hug.'

'Well, if the Lord has told you to do it, you'd better do it, but be careful you don't unbalance me as I could fall over.'

'No, I won't do that,' Maureen reassured me, and she awkwardly reached across my right shoulder, placing herself on either side of my right crutch, which my hand gripped tightly. My hand, my crutch, her crotch all in close proximity as Maureen did what she felt the Lord tell her to do.'

I had to laugh; this could only happen to me. I thanked Maureen for the prayer and swung through to the exit and the comfort of my car.

I reflected later as I shared with Jennie that there is inherent peril with this every-person collaborative ministry that was in vogue. The danger is that very willing and well-meaning untrained lay counsellors who are grasping for answers will inevitably wound unsuspecting miracle-needy people with their unwise, not-of-the-spirit counsel.

In the fog of my disappointment, self-pity began to fester more and choke the truth about my privileged place as an adopted child of the living God who promised me 'He would never forsake me. He who promises is faithful' (Hebrews 10v23).

What crept subtly into my spirituality was the theology of a distant, 'Him-up-there,' kind of God. My 'far away' creator God excelled in creating beauty and was majestically worthy of the praises we sang faithfully at Church services. From a distance, my God was awesome, and I would surely fall face down or remove my sandals, like Moses, if I were to encounter Him. But my new and distorted concept of Almighty God was lacking one vital truth.

Our spiritual foe has been prowling earth like a lion since the Garden of Eden. The 'father of lies' will twist truth in order to deceive us and blind us from one simple reality. Here is that truth: from the birth of time and Eden's walk, the creator, the Lord, is a personal God who invites us to walk with Him and to call him; 'Abba Father (dad) in Heaven.' Since the night that I knelt, as a young boy, at my bedside and opened my heart's door to him, I was adopted as his child, and no matter how hazy my faith had become, 'He remains faithful' (2 Timothy 2:11-13), this is personal.

Sadly, I was oblivious to this subtle self-pity-induced change. No longer was my God personal. Inwardly, I was frustrated with the life, the disabled life that had been forced onto me. I thought it was for a season and a reason, and here I was eleven years later with not a morsel of physical healing or understanding since the 30th May 1979. Spiritually, I appeared to be 'switched on,' I still prayed, I went to church, I still sang hymns and spiritual songs, but God seemed distant. I felt as if I was battling with this spinal injury, this paralysis, on my own, and now that I was married, I despised the restrictions it put on our relationship. It seemed unfair to impose this disabled life on my wife. I could not fulfil the most basic 'given' of a wedded couple…. I could not walk hand-in-hand with my wife, I couldn't dance, I couldn't accompany her to the lofty peaks in her beloved Lake District or show her the views from my favourite Slieve Donard where the Mountains of Mourne sweep down to the sea.

I felt sorry for her, but the festering yeast of self-pity was anaesthetising my passion for life and numbing my spiritual zeal and love for the Lord Jesus.

Shortly after the eleventh anniversary of Honister, I needed a break. I was five years into the sole proprietorship of my Chartered Accountants practice, employing four staff, and work was a-plenty. I was working twelve-hour days to keep abreast of the workload. Work pressure, lack of healing, too much voluntary work and the spiritual battlefield all combined to drive me to a personal low point, and Jennie put her foot down; 'We are going to the Isle of Wight for a break. I have arranged for us to stay at Alpine Road with John and Margie Wells.'

It was a significant trip and a turning point in my spiritual battle.

I had driven across the 'Downs' from the Fishbourne Ferry to

Ventnor many times since I first undertook the accountancy training at the Old Park Hotel, St Lawrence, in 1980, but this time, the Island's winding landscape of worked fields, ancient woodland and moorland began unwinding the tense human coil that I had become.

On the second afternoon at Alpine Road, I returned to the solitude of the bedroom to rest, pray and contemplate. Perched on the bedside chair, I tossed my limp legs onto the bed, transferred sideward and lay flat and stretcher-still staring upwards beyond the ceiling. After the eleven-year struggle with life and disability, I was having an emotional backlash. I was tired of bland assurances that God understood and that he would work all things for good for those who loved Him (Romans 8:28). As I stared Godward into the empty distance, the Lord, who was supposed to be closer than touch and as real as the air I breathed, seemed a million miles away. I was on an idyllic Island with my wife and friends, but the reality in that bedroom was that I felt utterly and miserably dejected and alone.

I began praying angry prayers, God-directed prayers and for all I knew, they were just thoughts bouncing off the walls and ceiling;

'Lord, you don't know how I really feel inside; God, you are an awesome creator, but can't you see my tears.'

'Jesus, you save my soul, you bore my sin, but you are doing nothing to mend my broken back, my broken dreams, nor my broken heart.'

'Our Father who art in heaven, you don't know me personally; you're supposed to interact, but you don't know how I feel. You don't see the tears I cry.'

'If you are all-knowing, if you are such a personal God, you would know I've had enough of this disability.'

'I've asked over and over again for healing. Jesus Christ, if you stood here in this room, I wouldn't just touch the hem of your garment; I'd grab your ankles and hold tight until you heal me. Lord, how can I get hold of you? You seem so far away; I feel like I'm in solitary confinement, and you've thrown away the key.'

My angry rant lacked reverence. It wasn't sugar-coated in King James Version liturgy or evangelical prayer jargon. The prayers were fuelled by pain and self-pity, but they were aching prayers of heartbreak, of longing and desperation. The contradiction of ranting to a distant God in such a personal way was ironic as my off-loading cast my cares on Him (1 Peter 5:7).

What happened after this changed my perception of God forever.

As I prayed, alone in that room, God responded deep into my heart with the spiritual precision of a surgeon's keyhole surgery. As I lay exhausted; emotionally and spiritually broken, I was lifted in a vision to a place I recognised and later to another place, I did not know. With a gentle firmness, God rebuked my rant with a crystal-clear visual response.

In my mind's eye, I was carried to the place where Jesus led his disciples after the 'Last Supper,' the Garden of Gethsemane. I could see myself in the garden. The evening sun lit the olive grove, creating shadows and soft shards of light. The trunks were gnarled, with branches reaching upwards to form an atmospheric canopy.

I was transfixed, out of sight, observing the disciples resting in the distance, and Jesus was there too, praying, dropping to kneel by a Mount Olive screed. Olive trees stooped over him and he was weeping as he prayed. Sobbing agony, blood droplets fell like perspiration from his forehead. I heard Him groan and pray. Faced with the cup of suffering he was about to imbibe. Ahead lay separation from his Heavenly Father, the cost of bearing the curse of humanity's sin; Jesus, aged thirty-three, my age, sobbed. Jesus wept in full knowledge that the Father would forsake a sin-laden Christ. His rib cage heaving and his chest pounding uncontrollably with tears from the very depths of his innermost self. I heard him roar, 'My Father if it is possible, let this cup pass from me,' I realised that these were not expressions of fear or pleas for mercy. This was a grieving realisation of what it meant to be devoid of God for even a brief moment in eternity, 'Father if it is possible, let this cup pass from me.'

Then, in my vision, Jesus paused mid-sentence, turned his head and locked his eyes on me. Me, Kelvin Burke in 1990 but mysteriously present in Gethsemane. Staring directly at me, Jesus continued, 'Yet not what I want, Father, but what you want.'

I was overcome with emotion, and I began to cry. Lying in that room in Ventnor, I sobbed, heartbroken, as I realised he did that for me, somehow 'before the foundation of the world' (Ephesians 1:4) and before the brutality of Good Friday, Jesus knew me, he understood my tears and my frustrations, and he walked forward from Thursday night's garden prayers onto Friday's crucifixion…for me. I was broken by this cosmic glimpse at reality… Jesus knew me, Christ knows me, he knows how I feel. I wept like I have never wept before, audible groans, tears like torrents, gut-wrenching, painful tears, healing tears.

Then, in the dream, I was carried from the garden, soaring like an eagle up and beyond a mountain range. From long distance, I could see beautiful lofty peaks and majestic shadowy valleys. Suspended face down, I hovered over one particular peak. As I looked, I noticed that it was, in fact, a crater, like an extinct volcano. Through my tears, I spoke to the Lord and said, 'Lord, why are you showing me a crater?'

The Lord said, 'Look into the crater.' I looked again and saw that the crater was not empty; it was filled with water.

'Lord, why are you showing me a crater filled with water?'

'Those are tears; that is a lake of tears,' the Lord replied.

'Tears?'

'Not one tear you have cried has gone unnoticed', He continued in a soft, tender voice, 'and for every tear you have cried, the Lord Jesus has wept ten-fold in the heavenly place. This lake of tears represents every tear that has trickled onto your cheeks; the Godhead knows them all.'

I had dared to accuse my Lord of being impersonal, unknowing, and distant, and here was my answer: he knows me down to my very last tear! The vision continued to unfold, and the Almighty revealed that not one tear has been lost, not yours, not anyone's. He showed me a scene of famine and starvation and affirmed that He wept ten-fold for the dry tears and hunger screams of starving adults and children. He knows that pain, too. I was broken by the revelation I received that day as I lay crying in my bedroom in Alpine Road, Ventnor. That morning, I wept in repentance, broken yet blessed. I sobbed in joy, yearning to know Him more intimately and to love him with all my heart.

Later, I read Psalm 56:8, 'You have kept count of my lament; put my tears in your bottle', and I took it as confirmation that this vision was of God. It was a defining moment, a life-changing experience that remains with me to this day. It taught me that I am known, totally, personally and loved unconditionally.

That God is a relational God, and I am an adopted son of a loving Heavenly Father. In truth, I find it hard to accept that God would adopt me as his own without some kind of servitude or, religious lifestyle or exemplary morality. But ten years after my Honister horror and more than twenty years after inviting Christ into my life, the penny dropped. Christians (and I am one) are God's own family, adopted, bought with the precious blood of Jesus and massively and absolutely loved as his own children – it's personal!

TEN

Business Matters

Alex Buchannan was known nationally as a 'pastor's pastor.' He had stayed in our home in Northern Ireland many times when I was a youth. He was a fearsome man, with a stern look accentuated by his left-side facial paralysis. We kept in touch after I moved to England. I felt privileged to come under his Godly influence and experience the weight of his piercing stare and probing examination in what he would call my 'spiritual MOT.'

I drove to York to visit my 'spiritual director' fresh from my Lake of Tears encounter. I shared with Alex that I had been transported to a realm that I could neither fully describe nor understand. All I knew was that God had resoundingly silenced my moaning and complaining that He was impersonal to my pain and ambivalent to the tears I cried.

In his inimitable direct way, he challenged me to 'stand and be the man' God has called me to be. To grow through the 'lake of tears' into a place of weeping with God in sharing his agony and longings so that he may 'bring through you his strong word in torrents of love, grace and mercy.' He continued in this prophetic way: the Lord asks, 'Where shall I find mighty preachers of righteousness that my will shall be accomplished?'

I resolved in my heart, as Alex spoke with me, to yearn for the anointing to preach God's word and to wrestle and pray over it, refusing to utter a word in sermonising unless I had spent time in God's presence to allow his living word to flow from my mouth.

It all seemed well and good when I was with my mentor, but it didn't take long for that yearning to be flattened by the mundaneness of life after soaring visions.

Encountering highs and lows in life, such as the 'lake of tears' experience and the Honister horror, can leave a false expectation that we coast from high to high and manage the lows by hoping for the highs. It is a mentality of 'living for the weekend' or 'looking forward to the holidays.'

After rising from the pit of self-pity and the 'Lake of Tears' experience, I settled into routine and accepted that most of life and living was quite ordinary and that the Lord promised to 'be with us always' on that journey. The 'rule of life' of a daily morning 'Quiet Time,' which included reading a bible passage and prayer and reflection, was vital spiritual sustenance for each day. Often, the reading for the day would provide content or narrative to the ordinary encounters of daily life, be it work, family, leisure or housing matters.

It seemed to me that most of Jesus' life was a story of interruptions and extraordinary happenings in an ordinary life.

True, miracles could hardly be called ordinary, but they happened in ordinary settings, like weddings, fishing trips, storms at sea, a disabled man at a swimming pool and a funeral cortege in Nain.

We had mini miracles to celebrate as we moved house from Sandal to College Grove in Wakefield. When we first married, we lived in my four-bedroom, two-story house in Sandal, the posh end of Wakefield. It was my first house as a young, able-bodied accountant. My father gave me a generous deposit that enabled me to gain the mortgage that got me onto the first rung of the homeowner's ladder. It was quite a homestead for a twenty-two-year-old.

Jennie agreed to move into my 'bachelor pad', as she called it, but a couple of years later, it was time for us to have a place of our own. Somewhere more sensible for a paraplegic husband, preferably with a garden or allotment for a green-fingered wife. A place where we may be able to start a family.

There was some drama in the ordinariness of the workplace. I completed my studies and qualified as a Chartered Accountant with the partnership that had been so supportive at the time of the car crash. I was surprised when John Fell, senior partner of the firm, summoned me to his office to let me know that I did not have a long-term future in the practice. His advice was that I should look for opportunities elsewhere.

In other words, they didn't need an eejit like me in their workforce, the years of blarney and messing about had caught up with me, and they were 'letting me go.' I didn't feel bitter; quite the opposite. They had given me a great start and thorough training in the world of business finance and stuck by me when hospitalised for the best part of a year, and I will always be grateful for that. Having talked the talk about trusting in the Lord, now was the time to walk the walk.

Proverbs 3:5-6 says to 'Trust in the LORD with all your heart; and lean not unto your own understanding. In all your ways, acknowledge him, and he shall direct your path.' When you are disabled and about to lose the security of work, bible verses can seem quite abstract. Pray as I tried, to 'cast my cares' on God because he cared for me (1 Peter 5:7) or to 'not be anxious about anything, but in everything by prayer … with thanksgiving let [my] requests be made known to God' (Philippians 4:6-7), I needed another job, and several of the interviews that I had endured were nothing short of disability discrimination.

One large Multinational engineering company in Leeds looking for a Chartered Accountant explained, after a promising interview, that they did not think I would be able to manage the amount of walking and travelling that was part and parcel of the job and, on that basis could not offer me the job. In this day and age, that would be called out as prejudice, but not in the 1980s.

A National heating and engineering company in Doncaster short-listed me, and as I sat waiting to be called for interview, the Managing Director sent word via his secretary that, if I could not climb the stairs to the interview room, I wasn't suitable for the job! I drove away from that disappointment, bruised and seething, that people could be so brutal and unprepared to give a chance to someone who was disabled but qualified and determined.

At this time, I had added to my rule of life the practice of Examen prayer. I would begin each day reviewing things to be thankful for, followed by a reflection on the previous day, asking the Holy Spirit to prompt fears and failings that needed to be brought to God in prayer. Each day, I would begin my journal with the word 'Yesterday….'

After the Doncaster incident, I wrote: 'Yesterday….. Lord, I adore you at the start of this day; I love you with all my heart and strength. Foul weather today cannot dampen my yearning for the One who holds my future, my hopes, my expectations, my job, and my all in his mighty hands.

I confess I was ill-tempered yesterday; I confess to not loving my enemy in the person of that hurtful MD. I confess to being in self-centred and self-pity mode, which I now detest, and ask God to cleanse me of this. I confess to being anxious when God cares and takes care of all my needs including my job. Lord, in your mercy and grace, forgive me.'

It was a good start to a new day, it was a way of letting go of those things that could have festered within me, leading me to grumble, write and complain with the all stress and time-consuming negativity that would ensue. There was no Disability Discrimination Act in those days that became legislation in 1995.

Fortunately, William Sugden's managing director, David Sugden, was prepared to take a punt on me. He phoned my referee, on the Isle of Wight, for an off-the-record chat about my state of physical wellbeing, and John waxed lyrical about my positive attitude to the paraplegia. It was an answer to prayer to be entrusted with the role of Company Accountant and Office Manager of Sugden's, a subsidiary of the Double Two Shirt Group. Established in 1869, Sugden's manufactured dress shirts, 'Jet' jeans and Topflight 'Threadneedle' workwear.

I still shunned the wheelchair and probably hopped a mile a day on crutches to fulfil my duties as an accountant and office manager. I loved the banter and interaction with staff, as well as my senior management responsibilities. I forged a good relationship with Double Two Chairman Isaak Donner. We were a multinational group employing over 1,500 people across six factories, but he ran the operation on the principles of a Market Stall. Cash Flow was king. Each morning he would wander into my office and say with his strong Austrian accent, 'What have we today?' By this, he meant how much cash have we got in? If my income was greater than the buyer's outgoings, it was going to be a good day.

Were I to protest and say we had record sales yesterday or that our cash received peaked yesterday, he would retort, 'If I am hungry this morning, don't tell me what I had for breakfast yesterday!' He was a wily old man, and it was best to keep on the right side of him.

Having the respected role of Accountant, I would sometimes issue bogus memos to office staff and factories. At least it amused me, even if it did get me in trouble from time to time. There was the time that I issued a memo to each factory Manager. In order to keep track of the number of toilet rolls each factory was using, every cubicle in factory toilets had to have a 'Toilet Roll Form' that was to be completed by employees before they left the cubicle. They were to enter the number of sheets they had used and add to the previous balance for a cumulative record 'for management purposes.' It nearly caused a riot in our Barnsley factory, and I confessed to irate Director John Sugden that it was, in fact, a prank. Other bad taste jokes have fortunately been lost to the Company archives, but I still get a smile from some of the craic we had. It got me a bit of a reputation as a 'crazy Irishman,' I hope and pray that it did not tarnish my Christian witness during my time as their Accountant. Hopefully, it portrayed that you could be a Christian and a Chartered Accountant and have a sense of humour!

After three fulfilling years in clothing manufacturing, I decided it was time to have a flutter on my own and Kelvin Burke &

Co., Chartered Accountants, was born, a small accountancy practice. My first client was Burke's of Cornascriebe, the family company formed by my grandfather in 1911. How that came about had a spiritual side to it.

My father asked me to present a Software Requirements Specifications report for his Tractor business. I dismissed Billy's request, knowing that I could not undertake the project while contracted full-time to Sugden's.

However, as I continued to engage in early morning quiet times, I found that I had lost a sense of peace or shalom. I couldn't put my finger on what or why this could be except that the words of the fifth Commandment kept coming into my mind; 'Honour your father and your mother.'

As kids growing up in Cornascriebe, we were brought up under the weight of the Ten Commandments, and number five was one we had quoted to us, usually at times of misbehaving. Honour seemed to us to mean duty, obedience and respect.

Being a 'bit of a lig,' my childhood was peppered with regular breaches of Commandment Number Five. The relationship I had with my father, 'Daddy,' was not tactile or tender except for my rear end, which was occasionally tender from tactile discipline! There were no hugs, no verbal, 'lots of love,' love was expressed through respect, obedience and duty. Nota bene, the mocking mnemonic 'rod.' My decision to leave Northern Ireland to study and then to remain in England for accountancy training was shrouded in an implied sense of 'dishonouring father and mother.'

After a time of discernment, I believed it to be a prompt of the Holy Spirit that I should accept my father's invitation to provide the evaluation with recommendations of the best computer package for 'Burkes'.' It would eventually bring a healing in my relationship with Daddy. Thus, Burkes of Cornascriebe' was the first client of Kelvin Burke & Co., Chartered Accountants.

Gradually, the firm became established in Wakefield in a salubrious area on the edge of Eastmoor Estate, where I had earlier been a Youth worker. Norma's sandwich shop and a turf accountant were my neighbours. Adjacent were the Rex Bingo and The Butchers Arms, with The Albion on the other side - refreshing watering holes. We developed a penchant for Nursing Homes, Self-Employed traders, Market Traders, vicars, 'subbies'- SC60s and all and sundry who had Irish connections. Many of my clients were rough diamonds who had to be honed to keep full and proper records of their trading practices. It was a joy to be a part of the local community, and ironically, we were about two hundred metres from St Andrew's Church.

Gradually, the accounting practice grew as did our reputation as a business of integrity. In some ways, it was more like extended family than business consultancy. Many clients became valued friends, and the guard of professionalism would drop as confidence and personal matters and concerns were shared. I found myself 'burdened' to intercede for the needs that were brought to my attention and prayed for opportunities to share the love of Christ with those I encountered each day.

Clients like Self-employed Stan, electrician and building maintenance sole trader was one of my first clients who became as close as a brother. I shared the good news of Jesus with him many times - how Christ lived the sinless life and died the sinner's death on the cross for us. Stan went on Alpha courses, Emmaus courses, Start, Just Looking, and Christianity Explored courses. I'm sure it was just to please me. He lived such a frugal lifestyle, foraging for wood and food, recycling and repairing people's cast-offs. He even wore my old jeans as his work clothes. Stan genuinely lived off next to nothing and was as honest as the day was long.

So, when the Inland Revenue decided to investigate his business because they said he was not drawing sufficient from his business to survive, I considered it a personal affront. I took his case on like a small-time lawyer to a BigLaw conglomerate. I prayed for both justice and mercy. The fees alone that accumulate from defending such an investigation can finish a small business off, even if the defence succeeds. Her Majesties Inspectors even stalked, sorry, followed Stan for a week but failed to reveal anything more than we had already stated in his full and proper accounts. I rejoiced on the day the Inland Revenue (now HMRC) finally accepted the accounts we submitted without any additional assessments or penalties.

Gordon was a real gentleman in both senses of the word. He was in business partnership with his wife Audrey. I had advised him very well on managing his hotel and minimising his tax bill, but I had never spoken to him about eternity, his soul, or his spiritual wellbeing. Would it be appropriate to mix faith and work?

When Audrey called in without an appointment to tell me Gordon had been diagnosed with cancer and had only weeks to live, it hit me like a bombshell. She wasn't just seeking advice about Inheritance tax when a partner dies; Audrey was crying out because she was broken and did not want Gordon or her daughter to know she was terrified of what may unfold in the weeks ahead. This encounter was pastoral rather than Accountant and client, and thoughts of codes of conduct or inappropriate blurring of roles seemed irrelevant.

I felt led to share with her a verse I had read that morning, 'Come to me you who are weary and heavy burdened, and I will give you rest (Matthew 11:28). I gave her these words of Jesus not knowing if I had overstepped the mark by mentioning faith when she was at a low ebb. I reassured her that I would be able to deal with her business and tax affairs in the event of Gordon's death. I also said I would be praying for them both and the family, and when I offered to say a brief prayer there and then in my office, she was moved to tears and said she felt more at peace and was grateful that she had called in.

As she left the office, I gave her a small booklet for Gordon. A dark silhouette of Jesus holding a crook stood out on the first page, 'The Lord is my shepherd.' I pointed to the word 'my' and said I want Gordon to know how close and personal the Lord can be to him through this walk through the valley of the shadow of death. I asked if I could refer him to my pastor, Rev John Ross, the minister at St Andrew's Church. Audrey consented, provided he was not a 'bible basher,' adding that it would also give Gordon the opportunity to talk about his funeral.

The following week, I arranged to visit the Hotel in Wrenthorpe with Rev Ross, and I was encouraged to see that Gordon was quite open and frank when he spoke with the vicar. I sat quietly as questions about preparing for eternity seemed more urgent than funeral preparations.

As John drew the meeting to a close, he said, 'Gordon, I'd like to leave you with a bible verse, something to think about in your quieter moments. My heart leapt as John quoted the same verse I gave Audrey a few days earlier. 'Coincidence or God-incidence?' Matthew 11:28: 'Come to me you who are weary and heavy burdened, and I will give you rest.' John wrote the verse on the cover of Warren's 'Journey into Life' and gave him the booklet to peruse.

As we drove back to the office on Stanley Road, I felt that God was affirming my decision to witness in the workplace when appropriate, and I prayed that there would be a 'coming together' through this verse as husband and wife faced an uncertain future together. Gordon and Audrey were included in the intercessions at St Andrews' Church Service on the following Sunday.

On Monday morning, a cheery Gordon telephoned, 'I've said that prayer in the book, I asked Jesus into my life, the 'sinners prayer.' I don't like the word sinner, but I know that's what I am. This is a fresh start for me; I just wish I had longer to live it out.'

The weeks became months, and Gordon's health was buoyed by palliative care and a new zeal for life. He died peacefully in Wakefield Hospice after putting his business affairs in order and leaving instructions for Rev Ross to conduct the funeral.

Not long after the funeral, I called to visit his widow. Audrey surprised me by saying, 'That's Gordon over there,' she nodded at the corner of the room where a deep-sea diver's shiny brass helmet was mounted on a wood plinth. 'His ashes are in an urn inside the helmet; I'm not sure what to do with them now.'

'We both know Gordon is not in the Urn,' I said.

'I know,' she replied, 'that book you gave him about 'the Lord is my shepherd' became a treasure to him before he died. He could say, 'The Lord is my shepherd' – it was personal to him.'

'Yes, Audrey,' I added, 'Psalm 23 concludes with words that say Gordon will dwell in the house of the Lord forever – and that is where he is.'

After a cup of tea and an emotional meeting, Audrey allowed me to say a prayer with her before I left. Driving back to the firm, I felt that something new had happened in the mundane everydayness of a Chartered Accountant practice; I had dared to vocalise my faith and the importance of soul Salvation with a client, and, as a result, eternity had been written on his heart. There was much rejoicing in heaven (Luke 15:7)!

At 86, Doris was my oldest and favourite client. She had been a widow for over 50 years. Her husband, a Baptist minister, had died of a heart attack after just nine years of marriage. She attended St. Georges C of E Church in central Leeds and was as radiant a Christian as I have ever known.

Doris didn't really need an accountant. A few dividends from stocks and shares were all that complicated her simple tax return. Each summer, I had the pleasure of visiting Doris, over a meal in a restaurant of her choosing, such as, Roundhay Park's Mansion Garden Room. The business matter in hand would take all of 30 minutes, concluding with a declaration signed by Doris, and then she could get on with the business of asking me how I was getting on with the Lord. It wasn't a scrutiny of the Alex Buchanan type, but a tender probing of a precious sister in Christ who genuinely cared for me and prayed that I would be more Christlike in all my dealings.

I shamefully admitted my loathing of HMRC because of Stan's tax investigation and similar cases. I knew she would have some wisdom to add to my personal reflections.

'The Lord knows your heart, Kelvin,' she said, 'your intention was not to sin. Perhaps you suffered the ignominy of the investigation because you take great pride in this word integrity.'

'Is there something wrong with that, Doris?' I objected.

'Well,' she lovingly answered, 'the Lord Jesus calls us to walk the path of humility that in all things he must have the pre-eminence always number one' (Colossians1:18). It is good that you want to be the best in your job and a man of integrity but sometimes we are brought low to learn that our pride gets in the way of Christ's pre-eminence. Even the best intentions and purest motives can deflect glory from Christ's pre-eminence.

I listened and learned and wondered how many times could someone fit this word I have never really bothered about into one conversation – pre-eminence - I realised Doris Roberts was on a deeper journey than I was. I yearned to be more Christlike in every way, not just the obvious things like Sunday church, daily prayers, Bible reading, and Christian music, but as John the Baptist once said, that I may decrease and Christ in me increase. That is a deeper spiritual level that dear Doris had opened my eyes to.

Three hours later and with a fee charge of 30 minutes, we left the 700 acres of parkland and lakes at Roundhay. I dropped this radiant sister back at her home in Headingly and headed South along the M1 to Junction 41. Back in the office in Wakefield, I mailed a very straightforward tax return to the Bradford office of Her Majesty's Inspector of Taxes. There would be no Inspector's enquiry on this one.

ELEVEN

Guided

On a personal note, we found out that Jennie was pregnant with our first child. Easter 1993 turned out to be very special indeed. Jennie and I could hardly contain our joy. We were keeping the news of the pregnancy to ourselves.

Discreetly, we went for the first scan, and our faces beamed as the obstetric sonographer confirmed our little one's heartbeat and gave us our first ultrasound glimpse of our child. Our joy was compounded moments later as the sonographer slid her transducer around Jennie's abdomen and casually said, 'Oh, there's two. You have twins!'

We were doubly blessed and thanked the Lord for these two little treasures that we were to be trusted with as parents. There was only one small problem: the back seat of a Ford Capri was not designed for two newborn baby car seats!

As I sat at the gate of the year 1994, I could not have imagined the changes that lay ahead. For nine days, it was just the two of us, then on the 10th of January, our twins, Chloe and Katie were born. We were a family of four, changes were afoot, and the accountancy practice was expanding and well-established in the area, but a surprise was in store. As Mini Hoskins wrote in her poem, 'The Gate of the Year,'

> 'Go into the darkness and put your hand into the hand of God. That will be to you better than light and safer than a known way.'

So I stepped into the year knowing Jennie would be a good mum and praying that I would be a good dad and a good boss for Kelvin Burke and Co. I did speculate, in my diary, when our twins were four days old, about how this world would develop.

> I wonder what will become of this world our girls are born into. Will technology advance to everyone having vision telephones, computers with video and TV combinations, Electric cars with electric filling stations? Will the UK return to Christianity by a revival, will we get back to God?
>
> —14 January 1994
>
> I had to go to work at 10 am through to 6.15 pm with a 2½ hr lunch break. This did not go down well; Jennie was extremely stressed and upset about the daunting task ahead of us.
>
> —17 January 1994
>
> I had a bad night with the girls, up at 3.30 am, feeding, changing, etc. Spent a gruelling day on Stan's Tax investigation at Pontefract Tax Office. Felt exhausted, went home at 6 pm and got told off by Jennie for being late.
>
> —18 January 1994

I was relieved when Peter Brookes and Catherine Chapman agreed to join the staff of my accountancy practice. Catherine was my PA at William Sugden's and understood my zany sense of humour. Peter was a rock-steady taxation specialist. There were now seven of us in the team, not huge in the big scheme of things, but big enough when it came to payday at the end of each month.

Increasingly, small accounting practices began to feel quite isolated and vulnerable as the larger firms began to merge into huge financial consulting conglomerates. I was blessed with a skilled staff who worked well as a team. Nonetheless, I was troubled in my Spirit about our vulnerability as a small company. In my quiet times, I began to seek guidance about the way forward for the practice. A reading from St. Paul's letter to the Colossians impressed me. Paul prayed that God would fill his readers with the knowledge of his will through all the wisdom and understanding that the Spirit gives (Colossians 1:9). I needed some of that! Over the years, I had come to rely on God-given peace about major decisions, prayerfully weighed up, and at this point in time, my peace was disturbed like concentric ripples on a smooth pond. Over the weeks that followed, as I prayed, I discerned God's voice saying that I was not going to be in accountancy until I retired. Consequently, I began to be more deliberate in my daily prayers about the business.

Apart from Jennie, I could not share or test my thoughts without risking a leak to my staff and clients about hypothetical mergers, which could unwittingly unravel the firm. I sought a clear word or sign regarding the future of the business. The only 'word from the Lord' was that my accountancy vocation would not be my occupation by the time I was of retirement age. Not much to hold onto at the age of 38. As I asked God for confirmation and direction, I wondered if this was merely a hunch or truly a prophetic word.

During the third week of September 1994, I signed up for a 'week of guided prayer.' The idea of a week of such intensity did not daunt me. During my formative years as a Christian I had attended several 'Prayer and Bible weeks' often led by my spiritual heroes Denis Clark and Alex Buchanan. However, this week, endorsed by the vicar of St. Andrews, Rev Bryan Ellis, was more countercultural than I had expected.

Firstly, it was led by a nun, sister Elizabeth O'Brien, a humble, wise Irish treasure from Cork. Secondly, it was based on an Ignatian Examen, Lectio Divina, which I had brushed off years ago as Catholic Mystic nonsense. Thirdly, it had a daily pattern of Bible study, prayer and an appointment with a prayer guide or spiritual director. Midst my busy life as accountant, husband and dad I wondered how could I commit to this Examen. Nonetheless, both Jennie and I signed up for the course, and it certainly illumined our path and directed our way.

Could this be a pattern that would be revelatory for me? My guide for the week was Sister Elizabeth. My Protestant prejudices were quickly assuaged as this slight, modest nun seemed to glow with the goodness and love of Christ. The way she held and leafed through and revered her Bible bore witness to the high regard she had for 'the living word.'

My exercise at the end of the first evening was to read John 1:35-39 and imagine I was one of the two disciples following in Jesus' shadow and then to dwell on Jesus' question to the two, 'What do you want?'

Having been a Christian for nearly 30 years, I had probably read the Bible from cover to cover about ten times, but I confess I had never dwelt or meditated on these few verses. I had digested the early verses of John 1:14, 'the Word became flesh and dwelt among us,' popularised in countless Christmas Carol services. I had read commentaries on and heard sermons on the deep meaning of John the Baptist declaring in John 1:29' the Lamb of God, who takes away the sin of the world,' but the gospel record of Jesus' first two, unnamed, followers had passed me by. Here I was under the spiritual direction of an Irish Roman Catholic nun, focusing on one insignificant verse: 'Turning round, Jesus saw them following and asked, 'What do you want?'

'As you pray over this scripture, Kelvin,' the siser added, 'imagine you are one of the two followers and allow yourself to answer the Lord Jesus when he asks this question, 'What do you want?"

'I'll give it a go.'

'Let's see what happens. Come back and tell me about it tomorrow,' Elizabeth enthused.

That evening, Jennie and I negotiated a half-hour of peace and quiet while the other juggled two demanding eight-month-old twins until slumber got the better of them.

My first foray into Ignatian spirituality was quite overwhelming. I had no preconceived response, but the raw ache of fifteen years of coping with paraplegia poured out. Jesus turned and saw me and asked, 'What do you want?'

I immediately said, 'Lord, you can make me whole; you are my only hope; I have no one else to turn to.'

In my imaginings, I noticed both compassion and sorrow in his eyes. Sorrow for the 15 years of waiting, seeking, and yearning and compassion for the deep, tender, tangible love he had for me. He repeated John's words and said to me, 'I am the Lamb of God; I died for your freedom, cleansing and healing.'

Tears were in my eyes, and a lump lay heavy in my throat as I said, 'Lord, how long must I wait for what I know you can do now?'

As I looked into his face, I saw that the Lord was weeping too as he replied, 'How long must I wait before lost people hear about me?'

As I related the half-hour encounter to Sister Elizabeth the following day, I realised my first reaction to Jesus' question was self-focused, and I wanted to correct that somehow. In prayer, I said, 'Lord, I want to be a trusted disciple of yours, one you can teach and impart your wisdom to, one you can rely on.' I continued, 'Lord, I want to be used by you to reach out to others for you.'

I felt totally drained by the end of the 'appointment' but so fulfilled and joy-filled that I couldn't wait to get my teeth into the next exercise. I was to read Revelation 3:14-21 and seek the Lord however he wishes to reveal himself through this well-known pericope, which finishes with the classic verse depicted in Holman Hunt's Light of the World, 'Behold I stand at the door and knock. If anyone hears my voice and opens the door, I will come in.'

Tuesday the 20th of September 1994 was an eventful day. I decided to work from home to complete the financial accounts for my own accountancy practice for the year ended 31st of July 1994, and late in the afternoon, I drove to Leeds with a draft Financial Statement, my workings and invoices for my auditor, John Dobson to finalise the accounts.

'Get them out as quick as you can, John, because I'm thinking of putting the business on the market'.

'Why would you sell up now when things are going so well?'

he replied.

We had just hit a record turnover, and there was common sense in his question. 'Why don't you continue for two or three more years of good growth and then merge with another small firm?'

I had worked with John when we were both at Neville Russell; he was a good Christian friend, and I valued his concern.

'I'm asking the Lord to clarify a word to me that I was not to stay in accountancy full term to retirement. I'm testing the market and testing the word. I'm prepared for every eventuality; I love the work, the staff and most of the clients, but I also want to follow the Lord's directing.'

In that unique situation of Christian brother and financial advisor, we prayed together that the Lord would indeed guide and direct me.

Earlier in the day, in my morning's quiet time, I engaged with the Revelation 3: 14-21 Ignatian exercise. It was equally as powerful as the previous day's encounter. As I read, re-read, and inwardly digested the passage for a third and fourth time, what opened up was very interesting. In truth, I never made it to the classic 'light of the world' text. Revelation 3:18 leapt from the pages and began a dialogue with God, during which I wrote fluently. My pen did not rest for 30 minutes.

> 'You say, 'I am rich, I have acquired wealth and do not need a thing,' but you do not realise that you are wretched. Buy from me gold refined in the fire so that you can become rich and white clothes to wear.' Revelation 3:17

As I dug deeper into the 'imagining,' I realised this was not about worldly riches but the gold of true faith refined in the crucible of life's experiences. The gold of abundant and eternal life was riches with which the financial wealth of an accountancy practice could not compare. I sheafed the Biro and knuckled down to completing my year-end accounts with fresh resolve to seek guidance from on-high about the way forward for the accountancy practice.

The dark oak church door of St Andrew's creaked at 8 pm as I leaned my shoulder against it to hop into the foyer for my appointment with sister Elizabeth. We avoided unnecessary pleasantries, like an Artic Tern, she swooped straight in, asking how I got on with the exercise.

'I am afraid I got stuck on verse 18.'

'The Lord often surprises us this way, directing us to an obscure verse that you may not have focused on before.'

I read aloud my Biro scripted Ignatian dialogue with God and re-lived the precious encounter of that morning. My eyes were moist with emotion as I looked up from my writing.

Sister looked directly into my eyes and said, 'Kelvin, the Lord wants to affirm the decisions you're making about your business.'

How could she say this, I wondered. I had not spoken to her about my conversation with John Dobson or the mental struggles I had been having about the future of the accountancy practice.

I inquired, 'What led you to say that to me?'

She replied, 'In my mind's eye, I got a picture of the rich young man in Mark 10:17-27. He stood before Jesus, the gaze of Christ looking steadily at him and loving him, saying, 'Come, follow me.'

'Kelvin, Jesus is looking at you and getting a response from you that pleases him.' This nun, who oozed gentleness and goodness, seemed unsurprised when I related to her that, a few hours earlier, I had been to my financial advisor and discussed selling the practice.

> First, a word from the Lord about selling the business and 'going for God.' It was uncanny talking to Sister Elizabeth. She spoke about the Rich Man selling up to go full-on for God, and I had not told her about selling my business! I felt this was a real assurance from God, that He was in control and knows the next step I need to take.
>
> — 21st September 1994

Psalm 16:7,8 was a recurring reassurance as I began the process of letting go of my business life and my livelihood. 'I will bless the Lord who guides me.... I know the Lord is always with me. I will not be shaken, for he is right beside me.'

LAKE OF TEARS

TWELVE

Called

On 28th April 1995, after much soul-searching, I finally agreed to sell the business to Peter, my Tax Manager. The transfer of the business was a real lesson in Proverbs 3:5, on trusting in the Lord, leaning not on your own understanding, and he will direct your path. That night, we packed our bags for another trip to our favoured welcome break - the Isle of Wight.

Later, as we sat on Sandown Beach, it was wonderful to see the twins tossing sand with their tiny spades for their first taste (literally) of sand and sea. This special island, with its apt motto, 'All this beauty is of God', was the right crossroads for me to reflect on the journey so far and to prophetically ponder the road ahead.

I had fended off countless suggestions that I was destined for full-time ministry. I contested using the conjecture of St. Teresa of Ávila that the Lord calls people to be his hands and feet, ears, eyes and mouth, where they are. We were all full-time ministers in the workplace, the tavern, the sports centre, the theatre - these were the places of encounter, our realm of influence, through which the Lord Jesus would touch the lives of others. Why would Jesus want to send me off to a 'vicar factory' to separate me from the exciting things that were happening where we were? Why would Jesus want me to wear a plastic dog collar around my neck, something that would set me apart, but not in a good way? That would put me on a pedestal or a pulpit – make me different – as if being a paraplegic wasn't enough! These were some of my protestations. It did not take much for me to launch into a right good rant about me never wanting to be a vicar.

On the final day of our stay on the Isle of Wight, I met with Eileen Wells in her Niton home, Greenbank, and shared a coffee with her.

It was 26th May 1995, and I sensed the Lord speaking to me through this godly woman. In conversation, she impressed upon me that it was more important to answer the Lord's 'call,' to be obedient and follow his leading than to stand on principle about 'clergification.' However, I do not think she used that exact word!

> Something clicked during the chat with Eileen Wells. I don't know what it was, but the Lord spoke to me through her. He wants me to train for ministry, but she thought that ministry would be different to that of a vicar in the parish. Jennie came over a bit weepy when we spoke about it, and we prayed together as we headed north again. I had a long time on the way up the motorway to pray in the spirit and seek: deep, gutsy prayers combined with a desire to worship, adore and commune with my Lord.
>
> —Friday 26th May 1995

The way ahead was still quite hazy; I was keeping my pact of taking time off one day per week to seek clarity and guidance. In the meantime, I successfully completed my Chartered Insurance Institute Financial Planning Certificate exams, which would open up the door to continue working as an

Independent Financial Advisor (IFA). The least I could do was to give God a hand in answering my prayer!

What do you do when you stop doing what you've always done? The cliche answer is you 'push doors' until one opens. But what do you do when several doors seem to open at once?

> I'm trying desperately to listen to what God may have in store for us, and I'm coming up with 101 hair-brained ideas that could work. It is a strange time for both of us - we feel in limbo.

—27th July 1995

My 'away days' were helping me draw closer to the Lord, and my Bible readings were precious and timely words that spoke directly to my inquiring heart. The process of writing prayers down kept my mind focused on the one who held my future, even if I could not fathom what that future held for me.

One such prayer in July 1995 went like this;

> 'Lord, help me sift through the ideas and openings I had so that I can clearly see the blessed path that you have chosen for me - give me a righteous boldness that perceives each moment as an opportunity given by you. May others see Christ in me.'

On another occasion in the calming ambience of the Yorkshire Sculpture Park, after reading Song of Songs 1:3, 'Pleasing is the fragrance of your perfume [Lord],' I wrote, 'I want to breathe in without exhaling... taking in Christ's fragrance and not let a single morsel out. Only in exhaling can I take more in, and in taking in and giving out, I become his pleasing fragrance. What a wonder.'

These 'in the desert' quiet times were rightly interrupted by the reality check of parental duties. One sunny summer's evening, things came to a head. The telephone rang, and Jennie was crying, almost bawling, 'There are two baby daughters here, with two dirty nappies and two empty tummies, and they need their father to be a daddy.' This was a different kind of aroma and an important challenge to what had become my tunnel vision for heavenly guidance and direction.

The New Year, 1996, ushered in a personal delight for our family: Jennie was pregnant again. Sadly, the joyful thoughts of a third child turned to despair in March when she miscarried. We journaled and clung to Bible verses and each other for strength as the same was sapped from us by our circumstances.

Psalm 42:3 'My tears have been my food day and night. Why are you down cast, Oh my soul? Why are you so disturbed within me? Put your hope in God, for I will yet praise him, my Saviour.'

One thing I have learned from these depths of sadness and incomprehensibility is that God is near, we are not forsaken, and the message of the 'Lake of Tears' is that he is weeping, too. Don't ask me how I know; I just know that turning to the divine when it doesn't seem to make sense enables us to collapse into his arms, to be held and carried through it all.

With some poignancy, Psalm 51:15 seemed to express my pain whilst desiring to praise, 'Oh Lord, open my lips, and my mouth will declare your praise. For you do not delight in sacrifice, or I would bring it. My sacrifice, O God, is a broken spirit.'

Jennie and I prayed together and talked about this personal heartache as those around us only saw a stoic façade. We felt unable to share our personal loss.

> The pain of loss today is immense. Have the chances of us having another child gone? That little soul is in glory worshipping our heavenly Father, and I never knew him (or her). Existed for a few weeks and now gone, it feels like a death to me, deep sorrow. In my

quiet time, I weep. I have given him into my Father's care, but the pain of never having held him is great. My comfort is that he is at the throne of the King of Kings tonight, glory be to God alone.

—21st March 1996

I continued to seek direction, and the idea of my 'calling' was beginning to raise its head.

> I have been thinking about a 'calling' and what the heck it is. I burn with desire to see people become thirsty for the fountain of Jesus, to seek and be found by him. I wonder if training will do me any good or if it will knock the passion out of me (surely, that could never happen).
>
> —Saturday 27th July 1996
>
> It is 6.30 am, the twins are up, I'm up.
>
> Happy Anniversary, darling. Jennie awoke like she had swallowed a wasp and made us all go back to bed for an hour. Not easy trying to convince two-year-olds it's not time to get up.
>
> Now, I am sitting in Seckar Woods, praying. I found a knoll in a tree trunk, and I sat and read the bible and prayed for an hour.
>
> The sun is pushing through the beech trees onto the bare undergrowth. It was a good prayer time; I read the Fishers of Men passage – Matt 4:19. I received no guidance, no message.
>
> —Friday 2nd August 1996

The 9th of September 1996 was a grey, drizzly day, and I decided to seek cover in a retreat house in Hepworth for more of the same, seeking but not finding answers. The barns, converted into a Hermitage, had been recommended as 'always open' and welcoming for personal contemplation. Except, unsurprisingly, for the day of my visit, the door was closed. I was locked out. Undeterred, I nestled in against the white-washed walls, sandwiched between a profusion of crimson red geranium plants. With the distinctive scent of geraniums ascending, I sat like a stooge on a Mediterranean travel brochure. There I lounged in the cold, resting my callipered legs on two rims of geranium-filled terracotta pots and prayed aloud,

'Lord, do you want me to get ordained or not? Do you want me to go to Bible college to study or not?'

I did not expect an audible reply, and I wasn't disappointed. My eyes dropped to Psalm 25:4 as the rain began to fall heavy, 'Show me your way, Lord, teach me your path, guide me…for you are my God, my Saviour, and my hope is in you all day long.' Soggy and cold, I locked my orthotics, hopped to my Ford Capri and headed home.

An eventful two years had passed since Rev Bryan Ellis had invited the Ignatian prayer guides for our first week of Lectio Divina guided prayer. On 1st October 1996, Sister Elizabeth was back with a new team of listener guides. Jennie and I enrolled once again. The Examen process had deepened my times of reflection over the last couple of years and I anticipated another precious time off growing in faith. I could never have predicted what actually transpired.

I was disappointed that Sister Elizabeth was not to be my prayer guide for the week. Brenda was 'assigned' to me, and I assumed she was a Sister living in the same convent as Elizabeth.

At 9.30 pm, I was the last of Brenda's appointments for the day. At the end of the second day's feedback from the Examen exercise, I exchanged pleasantries with Brenda: 'Are you off back to the convent at Huddersfield now?'

'I Don't live in Huddersfield; I live at the Hermitage in Hepworth.'

'Oh, that's weird,' I replied, 'I was there three weeks ago for a quiet, reflective day, but it was closed.'

'It's always open,' she said.

'Not the day I went, so I just sat outside with the geraniums and prayed.'

Brenda's eyes startled with emotion as she said to me, 'I don't know if this will mean anything to you, but I was bringing the plants indoors this morning to protect them from the frost, and as I picked up one of the geraniums, two words came to me.'

'What were they?'

' "Kelvin Ordination", it was very clear, almost audible.'

I was stunned to silence and slowly related to Brenda that I had been seeking guidance for two years and that I had asked the Lord midst the distinctive scent of these very same geraniums just three weeks previously – 'Lord, do you want me to train for Ordination?'

I was trembling under the power of what was happening, the realisation that this was the answer to the question I asked of God twenty-two days earlier. It doesn't get any clearer than this, 'Kelvin Ordination.'

Brenda could not have made it up. There were no hints in my Ignatius imaginings over the two short sessions that I had met with her. Truly, I had prayed that bold prayer in Hepworth, and then the rain began to fall. In fact, I had even forgotten the details of the prayer except for the record in my journal on that dull day in the parish of the Holme Valley.

Back at home, I was telling the story to Jennie when the telephone rang. It was the Rev Bryan Ellis. he said he wanted to come round and talk to me again about 'ministry.' This seemed to emphasise the reality of the 'calling.'

Two days later, on 4th October 1996, Rev Ellis came to see me and said that he had been praying about our previous conversation in July. He said he would like to refer me to the Wakefield Diocesan Director of Ordinands (DDO), Felicity Lawson, and recommend me for ordination training as a Church of England minister. Things were developing so fast that I could hardly take it in. After two years of asking, waiting and wondering, in just two days, I was arranging to meet the Bishop of Wakefield's DDO with a view to CofE ordination – crazy!

The Reverend said prophetically that he thought, one day, I would be the minister of St Andrew's and St Swithun's churches. I protested, saying that Jennie and I did not think we would be staying in Wakefield.

He offered half a smile as he said, 'We will see.'

By the end of the year, I had met with the DDO and was an ordinand in waiting. Meanwhile, in the County of Armagh, Presbyterians Billy and Rita Burke were none too excited about the prospects of their son being a priest in the Church of England. Nonetheless, I was convinced the geranium story was not a coincidence; it was more like a 'God instance,' it was a 'call.' As such, I began the process of answering the call, not knowing what the journey ahead might be like, but I felt assured that it was to be my new vocation.

It took me a while to settle into the routine of ministerial training at Cranmer Hall, St John's College, Durham University. The lectures were just a part of the whole caboodle. I enjoyed getting my teeth into Biblical Theology, New Testament studies, Old Testament studies, Church in Society, PTM (Payer Theology and Ministry), Worship, Preaching and Communication, Systematic Theology, Liturgy, Church History and Ethics. Hebrew and Greek were not my favourites.

My first year 'placement' was a dream ticket. I dreaded a hospital chaplaincy posting. I had spent nine months of my life incarcerated in hospital following my accident, and I had no yearning to spend my Wednesday afternoons or Sunday mornings at the University Hospital of North Durham, aka Dryburn Hospital. I felt blessed to be assigned to Reverend Alan Farish, the minister of the Arts Centre, a church plant in Fatfield Estate, Washington.

Alan was an effervescent Christian evangelist who radiated a personal faith. Tragically killed in an accident in 2019, Alan was foremost a pastor, trainer, evangelist, and mentor who enabled others to flourish, often to the lessening of himself. During the second week, whilst I was at college, he visited Jennie to reassure her that the congregation at Fatfield would embrace our family as part of the placement. It was a thoughtful act that extended a welcome to the whole family. We were officially introduced to the Arts Centre church on 19th October 1997. It was a wonderful welcome for all four of us. Consequently, we settled into the fellowship at Fatfield, not ticking the 'placement' box but belonging and feeling affirmed and valued as a whole.

Fifteen meaty essays, two video sermons and two sweaty exams later, I had progressed through the vicar factory, having learned to regurgitate library books and journals and wax lyrical about Hilda at Whitby, Arius, and Augustine, to name a few.

Jennie had also progressed through the stages of a pregnancy that began in secrecy. I feared the DDO would delay my training by a year. In truth, Ellie's birth was untimely for a number of reasons! Many of the deadlines for end-of-year assessments fell in the month of May and as usual, I was taking it to the wire before submission. In addition, I had preaching commitments and the Alpha Course at the Arts Centre. There was also the distraction of Chelsea FC playing in the European Cup Winners Cup final on 13th May.

On 10th May, I was preaching at the Arts Centre on 2 Corinthians 1:20, 'God's 'Yes' is in Jesus.' It was such a privilege to speak about Jesus being 'yes' to all God's promises after eight people from our Alpha course had said 'yes' to Jesus by going forward for baptism and confirmation.

Ellie kept us waiting, her little head peering with wide eyes out to the world four minutes before she wriggled her torso and legs into the beckoning world. She was born at 3:03 pm on 13th May, weighing four bags of sugar or 7lb 13ozs to be precise. It was worth it all as I held my newest infant, staring in amazement at the miniature pink fists and tiny toes curled this way and that on flatter feet.

Ellie was introduced to the fellowship at Fatfield Arts Centre the following Sunday. Alan Farish called all of us to the front of the auditorium and asked me what the happiest moment of the week was: Ellie's birth or Chelsea winning the Cup. To which I replied, 'That's a difficult question, but the baby's middle name is 'Zola!' The Italian Gianfranco Zola had scored the winner at 9.30 pm to end a perfect day.

On 17th September 1998, I received an invitation from the

PCC of St Peter's Stanley, West Yorkshire, to assist their vicar, Bill Henderson. I had attended St Peter's morning service the previous Sunday and felt warmth and welcome from the congregation. I duly accepted their invitation of a curacy in Stanley.

In the words of Willy Nelson, we were, 'on the road again,' Wakefield was our destination, St Peters, Stanley our church and our own house in Barratts Road was our vicarage. After two years at the vicar factory, we were heading home. God is good.

THIRTEEN

Homecoming

Five weary travellers pulled off the A642 and stared apprehensively at the monstrous twin towers of the coal-stained York stone of Saint Peter's, Stanley. The occasion was the Bishop's Millennium Service, 'Christ our Light', when the congregation would be commissioned to take 'the light of Christ into the next Millennium.' Bishop Nigel brandished a three-foot candle and branded each disciple with a metal flame badge as we prepared for the next century.

After two years of training at Cranmer, I wasn't sure what a curate actually did, six days per week for three years. Fortunately, Rev Bill Henderson had an induction plan. 'Sunday is a working day. Monday is a day off.' That was a good start. Over the next three years, we hatched a schedule that would introduce me to parish ministry. It all seemed a bit daunting at first, and I owe a lot to Bill for his gentleness, inexhaustible patience, and encouragement from the start. He was sound, solid, wise, and unflappable, with a sense of perspective that grounded his faith in a daily walk with the

Lord and with the people he served – his diaconate. There was plenty of craic, as we say in Ireland, in the three years that we worked together.

Wakefield Hospice was in our parish, and the vicar suggested that I introduce myself to their chaplain. I duly engaged with the staff there and was appointed honorary chaplain. Each week, I looked forward to those encounters. People with life-limiting prognoses would often allow the 'spiritual stranger' to draw alongside them to share their story and welcome the Holy Spirit's gentle whisper.

My first pastoral visit to Pinderfield's Hospital was with Suzie. She had been an active member of St Peters church for over 50 years. She had been admitted to Pinderfield's Hospital and asked for a visit from the 'new curate.' As I sat and listened, engrossed in Suzie's life story, that of a beautiful effervescent Christian, I felt the Lord affirming in my spirit, 'This is why you have been called.' She spoke fondly of meeting Stanley miner Norman, who was stationed in the Cotswolds in WW2. Suzie had served on St Peters PCC, WI, Ladies Society and was devoted to her Lord Jesus. Now hospitalised, nearing the end of her earthly life, Suzie wished to share the Eucharist one last time.

As I opened my portable communion kit and carefully laid the white linen purificator on her bedside table, she fell silent. As each implement- the patten, chalice, and cross was placed on the cloth, we both sensed it was indeed a holy space. We joined together in the familiar words, 'Heavenly Father, we do not presume to come to this your table trusting in our own righteousness.' Then we said the Lord's Prayer and shared the broken bread, intincted in wine and thanked the Lord for feeding us. Suzie's face glowed like an Angel as we shared this holy moment at her hospital bedside. I kissed the back of her hand, holding back my tears. I had been blessed by this saintly lady, and my hospital phobia was long forgotten.

A few weeks later, there were more droplets for the lake of tears as I stood at Suzie's graveside in Stanley, leading family and other mourners in prayer as we committed her to God's merciful care. Surely, her name is in Heaven's Book of Life.

Three years at Stanley flew past, and it was time to move on, but what to and where to? Jennie and I spent many a long evening in our beautiful Barratts Rd home pondering where we would end up. We were also exploring parishes in the Carlisle Diocese. Bishop Graham Dow had encouraged me to look at churches in Silloth, Barrow-in-Furness, Penrith and Brough. My Father's Parkinson's and father-in-law's heart condition were a constant concern. Carlisle was a good deal closer to Northern Ireland than Wakefield.

I flew to Belfast to meet the Bishop of Down and Dromore – Harold Miller, and the Dromara and Annalong interregnums got my family all excited about the prospect of wee Kelvin moving back to the Emerald Isle. Before flying back to Yorkshire, I spent an hour at St Anne's Cathedral in Belfast, praying in the South Transept for clarity and guidance.

I meditated on Psalm 25 - it echoed the longings of my heart. 'In you, Lord my God, I put my trust, (v4) show me your ways Lord, teach me your paths, guide me in your truth and teach me, for you God, are my Saviour and my hope is in you all day long.'

There was no neon sign saying – 'this is the way,' but the Shalom-peace was in trusting the Lord and knowing, at the right time, he would reveal to where and to what we should go.

Back in Wakefield, I met with the Chaplain at Pinderfields Hospital, who spoke about an opportunity in healthcare chaplaincy coming up if I was interested.

My head was spinning with all this talk of opportunities and doors opening. I was dreaming and dreading, in equal measures, what lay in store for us. The only thing we knew for sure was that we would be moving. Jennie and I were not at peace with each other on which doors we should push.

> Met with Bishop David this morning, he said 'no' to extending the curacy by 12 months to be seconded to St. A's. I feel gutted. Jennie had a word from the Lord: 'Wait and trust the Lord.' I wish I did. I've been to Hospital for Chaplaincy, a bit deflated but the patient encounters picked me up. Afterwards, I gave a man a lift to the bus station, he stunk of alcohol. I thought he could be an angel with a word from God to me! Nothing doing, he wanted a fiver!
>
> —Tuesday 7th May 2002

Throughout my final year at Stanley, Bill Henderson had released me from time to time to serve and support St. Andrews Church during their long interregnum. Often, in these times of servitude at St Andrew's, I was strangely moved to tears. I could not explain the source or reason. Even on joyous occasions, like Tom Rishworth's Baptism or the Easter Sunday service, for no apparent reason, I was welling up with tears. It was as if I could feel or sense their pain, the sadness of several years without a pastor. In hindsight, I know it was God's gentle whisper that this was to be my next move.

There was no prophetic word or guiding star, but the tears spoke to my heart that we were to serve the Lord at St Andrew's. It was the church where I had been the youth pastor, it was in the parish where I had been incarcerated in a hospital for eight months, it was the church where I had met, and in 1986 married Jennie, and it was on the same road where my accountancy practice was based. It seemed the perfect fit.

The icing on the cake was that the 'move' was not a move at all. We did not have to up sticks and leave our bungalow; there would be no uprooting from school for our three girls – no upheaval of relocating. The vicarage was our own house. The Bishop of Pontefract sanctioned it, and by God's grace, we were on to homecoming part two.

Bishop David James conducted the licencing at St. Andrews on 10th July 2002. He and his wife Gill had been so supportive during my curacy and worked hard, behind the scenes, to make this appointment. We met at his 'Lodge' a few days before the service, and I chanced my arm and brought up the subject of vestments.

'Bishop, do I have to wear those wretched robes at the licencing?'

'What would you like to wear instead, Kelvin?'

'I am more comfortable in a smart suit than liturgical robes.'

'Okay, we will both wear a suit for your induction service.'

What a guy, such humility – the Bishop was prepared to accommodate the wishes of the church and the incumbent in this low evangelical parish.

In contrast to the sombre Victorian mother church, St Swithun's Church, in the heart of Eastmoor Estate, was an uninspiring poor relation. Fortunately, the previous incumbent, Rev Bryan Ellis, had graciously agreed to its demolition. That sparked the formation of the Eastmoor Community Project in 1996 and the building of the St. Swithun's Centre, which was nearing completion in my first few months as vicar.

This innovative centre was the parish office and the base that I chose to work from. Everything was new and pristine. There was an air of positivity around the creation of this hub for the community. The building was more like a spaceship that had descended from a Spielberg movie than a centre for a community that had suffered following the closure of Parkhill Colliery in 1983.

In short, being a vicar is very different to being a curate. You need the wisdom of Solomon, the patience of Job, the courage of David and the health and strength of Samson all rolled into one clergy. There are many situations where you know the buck stops here, and there are plenty of people to remind you of that fact. I would need to call on the support of my spiritual director – Sister Elizabeth, and I wanted to stay close to Bill Henderson, my training incumbent in the neighbouring parish in Stanley. It is vital in this unstructured life of parish ministry to keep a sensible work-life balance; prioritising family needs alongside the demands of church, parish and diocese. I did not always get it right, but I did try.

It was so encouraging to see the green shoots of growth pushing through the rough terrain of this 13,000-peopled parish. A local non-conformist church, Destiny, asked if they could hold their Sunday afternoon services at St Andrew's. That was a blessing, and the camaraderie between Pastor Ian Critchley and I gave mutual spiritual support.

The vibrancy of parish ministry was shattered on Monday, 16th December 2002. We had two wonderful Sabbath day services the day before. A nativity play at St Andrew's where children adorning tea towel head coverings and toggle-held sheets brought the Christmas story to life. St Swithun's Centre hosted a 4 pm 'Christingle', which was packed with Eastmorians eager to pick the sweets off the red-ribbon-clad oranges.

It was an excellent start to the Christmas program.

The telephone rang at 9 am, it was David Harpin, Funeral Director; 'There has been a double murder on Park Lodge Lane, mother and daughter, you need to get up here.'

That one phone call changed the course of the whole week and soured the festive season.

I arrived at the crime scene shortly after. It looked like a setting for a film shoot. The police cordoned off the area, a white forensic tent, to enter the flat. Several satellite-laden outside broadcast trucks with journalists on the loose. I hopped confidently on orthotics and crutches towards the two constables who were securing the area for the crime scene investigators.

'I am the vicar of the church round the corner; I wondered if I could help in any way?'

The young constable replied respectfully, 'Morning Reverend, I met you yesterday at the Christingle. I'm afraid you will not be able to help here, but I can ask the neighbours for you. They have been traumatised by everything they heard at 4.00 am this morning.'

I thanked him for recognising me and thought it was amazing that I already had a link with one of the officers at the scene. It helped me relax and focus. What could a clergyperson do in such a situation? When I was training at Durham, we had a session on responding to major incidents, but this was the real thing. The was no time to consult seminar notes - I was in the deep end with one friendly copper to hold my hand.

'By the way,' he continued, 'the T.V. journalists are about to descend on you.'

'What behind me now?'

'Yes, you will be on live T.V. My suggestion is to tell them what a great area this is and that this tragedy is out of character for your parish.'

What a timely piece of advice; I had seconds to gather my thoughts before being broadcast on worldwide news channels.

'Can you give us your thoughts on the two murders last night, Reverend?'

Several microphones were thrust towards my face.

'This is totally out of character for Eastmoor. I am in my first year as vicar here, and I have nothing but praise for the way people on this estate support each other. This is a peace-loving community that will be shocked that two of their own could be attacked in such a way.'

'What about the little boy? He was in the flat?'

'I am not aware of the details, but I'm sure there will be a groundswell of support for him.'

'Thank you, Reverend.'

That tragedy started a chain of encounters that would thrust me into the lives of people who would willingly admit to not being 'religious.'

I spent the next couple of hours visiting the residents of the flats. The couple in the flat below the crime scene wanted to talk. Ironically, the man had been to a funeral I conducted for a friend of his in Stanley. The lady in the adjacent flat remembered me from the time when I was a youth worker on the estate - her daughter came to the church youth group.

The following day, I met a brother of one of the deceased. Later, I met a cousin of the other victim. When I met the grandfather of the three-year-old, I was reassured that the little boy was in the care of his family. I offered prayer to the bereaved. No words of comfort would be sufficient to ease the pain of their loss and brutal separation. Prayer draws us into the presence of our Father in heaven, who cannot change the situation, but he can change us if we open our hearts to let him in.

Everywhere I went throughout that week, the words on the lips and thoughts on hearts were for that family and especially the little boy. People would stop me and give me money for his care. We started a Post Office Savings fund where people could donate for his future support. I remained involved because the family did not wish to speak to the press directly. Thus, I became a buffer between them and an inquiring public. Most of the time, it was well-intentioned but nonetheless overpowering for a family in shock from the trauma. I felt privileged to be trusted in that way. Hundreds gathered weeks later for the double funeral of mother and daughter; two coffins lowered into one grave - together forever - it was a real heartbreaker. I felt that God had guided me throughout this major incident. First, Harpin's telephone call, then the constable assisting me with the media melee, the encounters in the neighbour's flats, being able to speak with the family and then conducting the funeral in a way that honoured their loved ones. Finally, the little boy had Post Office savings with donations accumulating financial provision for his future.

A few weeks later, I caught the train to spend a couple of days in the garden cottage at St Anthony's Priory. It was the perfect quiet place after a time of turmoil. The splendid gardens, with Durham's magnificent cathedral and castle as a backdrop, were an oasis to my weary soul. Spiritual Director, David Bosworth sensitively guided me through the scriptures to cast my cares on the Lord.

I returned to the parish refreshed and rebooted to serve the Lord and the Wakefield Diocese. The two bishops who had influenced me greatly, Nigel and David, had moved on, and bishops Steven Platten and Tony Robinson were consecrated - they were my new pastors.

The Park Lodge Lane murders had stirred us up as a fellowship, we could be good neighbourly. New faces were showing up at church week after week. We ran outreach courses such as Alpha in the new upstairs conference room on 29th September 2005. There were twenty registered inquirers for our Alpha supper. Over the duration of the exploration, some were coming to faith and others - just looking.

I loved being a minister in an inner-city estate. As I entered the final year of my contract as priest-in-charge at St Andrew's and St Swithun's, I knew I would miss the precious everyday encounters with parishioners just as much as the Sunday Services. I relished the banter with those for whom the church was irrelevant, the warmth of those who welcomed me into their lives at times of bereavement, illness, exorcisms, baptisms and weddings and the regular 'bumping-into' former accounting clients and ex-youth club members.

Throughout my time in Stanley, followed by Eastmoor, Wakefield, I could not deny that the highlight of my weekly routine, 'on the beat,' was my time in healthcare chaplaincy, be it hospice, hospital or care home visiting. As the church and diocesan office began the process of reflecting on my five-year tenure, I was also reviewing and seeking guidance about a different course.

On a hot summer's afternoon, I sat in Pinderfield's Hospital Chapel after visiting on the Spinal Injuries Unit, and I sought the Lord for direction. Unbeknown to me, the prayer was already being answered. Matthew 6:8 says, 'God knows our needs before we ask.'

Concurrently, at home in Barratts Rd. Jennie was seeking an answer to this same prayer. In her spirit, she felt led to look on the Church Times website, where she spied an advert for a job in the Chaplaincy Department at Leeds Teaching Hospitals NHS Trust. My interest sharpened after a telephone conversation with Rev Dr Chris Swift the following day.

Word was coming from Northern Ireland that my Father's health was deteriorating, and a conversation with the Bishop of Down and Dromore encouraged me to think of moving back to Ulster. It coincided with news of Dad's health. What was I to do? Where was God leading, Chaplaincy at Leeds or 'home' to Northern Ireland?

It troubled me greatly that my relationship with my dad, whilst always being respectful, was not tender or loving in a demonstrative way. Despite living in Yorkshire and he in Northern Ireland, we spoke often and were civil with each other but more like mutual customers than Father and son. I adhered to the Fifth Commandment but merely paid lip service to it. I knew I had to do something about it and booked several flights from Yeadon Airport to Belfast over a period of three months.

On these visits, we would sit and talk about things past and present. You could call it 'the long goodbye.' It was precious quality time; I could sit for hours and ramble on, but I could not tell him that I loved him. I could thank him for the years of support and countless gifts and his kindness and generosity - words of appreciation, but could I put my arm around him in a loving embrace and say those words? No Sir, it was like my Adam's apple was on strike and I had selective arm paralysis.

Having cancelled our plans for my fiftieth birthday, I sat with Billy Burke on 28th May 2006. He was frail and stooped, his Parkinson's disease had reduced his walk to a shuffle and his tremor and swallow were so bad we had to spoon-feed him at mealtimes. He still had the light of 'the boss' in his eyes, and his dry sense of humour was undeterred. His once commanding voice was now a decibel above a whisper as he said: 'What do you think of me?'

'Do you mean your health - your Parkinson's?'

'Aye, what else could I mean?'

'I think you're remarkable. You keep going.'

'How will your mother manage when I go?'

'We will be there for her, us three boys.'

We were sat outside the Cornascriebe house on a rickety cast iron bench. Dad's friendly, full-plumed Peacock ambled serenely by. We looked down the lawn to the 'Pony field' and beyond. I was bursting to speak affectionately to him as he said,

'I'm worried about her.'

I could feel the anguish of a man about to say his last hurrah to his partner of fifty-five years without knowing the right words to say.

'Tell her you love her, and all will be well,' I ventured. I swallowed the lump in my throat and said, 'I want to say something to you. It's something I have never said before.'

'What's that?' he whispered.

'I love you very much,' I broke down and wept, and he interjected,

'Sure, I know that; what are you telling me that for?'

'Because I have never said it before, I want you to hear it from my lips and know that it's true. I do love you, and I'll be heartbroken when you die.'

His voice was cracked and broken as he said, 'Well, it has to happen sometime.'

He was fighting back his own tears as we sat in silence for long enough. I felt relieved of my burden. I regretted that it had taken fifty years to express it verbally, but I sensed a real peace and a newly won koinonia between us.

My brother Richard chauffeured me to George Best Airport for the flight back to Leeds.

'How did you get on with Dad?' He asked.

'I told him I loved him.'

He virtually did an emergency stop, 'Boys-a-dear, how did you manage that?'

'I just came out with it.'

'That's tarra; it's something I wish I could do.'

'Well, it's just something I had to do.'

We left it at that.

As I accelerated along the runway for take-off, I placed my

trust in God and gave thanks for my Ulster roots and my English tribe – Jennie and the girls. In an hour, I would touch down to the stress and strains of a minister in an inner city parish.

My dad went to be with the Lord the following day, just after midnight on 30th June 2006. Remarkably, or providentially (take your pick), I had just used my last pre-booked flight ticket to fly back to the province for the mini-breaks at Cornascriebe. I returned to Yeadon at midday on 29th June 2006.

Twelve hours after I embraced Billy Burke in a fond farewell, his Lord Jesus welcomed him to the heavenly place he had prepared for him for all eternity (John 14:6).

FOURTEEN

Chaplain

It was a balmy summer's afternoon in 1984 in Hacienda Heights, Los Angeles when pastor Giff Claiborne spoke prophetically to me. He broke off from his prayer and said, 'Kelvin, you will be involved in the healing ministry.'

On the 22nd of August 2006, twenty-two years later, the not-so-famous 5, we're heading south on the M1 motorway. We were destined for a week's vacation on our beloved Isle of Wight. The mobile phone rang, it was Rev Dr Chris Swift of Leeds Teaching Hospitals NHS Trust, 'We want to offer you the job of hospital chaplain.'

After I accepted the offer, he asked me to enrol at St. Michael's College, Cardiff University for their three-year Master of Theology, with specialism in Healthcare Chaplaincy.

'Definitely, it will be a privilege.'

I hung up and whooped with glee. Our three backseat drivers had not seen such childish exuberance from their dad.

'I think you're happy, Dad,' said Katie, understating as usual.

'Does that mean we have to leave church?' asked Chloe, thinking of friends as usual. 'Yes, it does.'

'Where will we go to on Sundays?' pondered Ellie, now eight years old.

'We will find somewhere,' replied Mum, 'this is a new job for Daddy, working in hospitals.'

Another period of seeking guidance had ended. The Lord had opened the doorway to Healthcare Chaplaincy. I was to be a member of the spiritual care team at Leeds. The multifaith department of twelve included; Jewish, Christian and Muslim chaplains plus an army of volunteers to support those, in our care, of all faiths and no faith. Holistic care extended to staff, patients and the wider family connected with the trauma and illness.

Leeds Teaching Hospitals in 2006 was the largest NHS Trust in the U.K. and stretched across seven sites. What a place to cut my teeth as a rookie healthcare chaplain. With our payroll of nearly 14,000 staff and several thousand volunteers, this felt like a calling to minister in the equivalent of a small town, not to mention the patient-centred care of those occupying the 1500 beds and many daycare centres.

I managed to convince the panel of St. Michael's College, Centre for Chaplaincy Studies that I had sufficient sensibility to be accepted onto their three-year Master of Theology degree course. It was back to the world of academia for me.

There is no way that I could be described as an academic; my college tutor said I wrote like a tabloid journalist rather than a scholar. I took that as a compliment. Now enrolled as a post-grad student at Cardiff University, I could wheel out phrases like 'human flourishing,' 'benevolence and beneficence,' 'reflexive and reflective practice,' 'ambivalence and emotivism' with a smattering of Greek and Latin thrown in, to get by in this seat of learning where I did not really belong. It was a privilege to be in this beautiful college for four residentials per annum, mingling with chaplains of all genres: Ministry of Defence, H.M. Prisons, Education, Industry and, of course Healthcare. The tranquillity of the gardens and the distinct modernist Chapel was a sanctuary I would be paid to attend over the next three years.

The world of healthcare chaplaincy is very different to the world of a parish priest. For a start, you are on the payroll of a secular paymaster, the NHS, and that brings with it certain constraints for the zealous Christian. There can be no proselytising. Nonetheless, a patient or staff member would often make faith inquiries, which led to salvation. Another is that the parish is replaced by the population of the hospital and its catchment area. The working day is flexible but still has the structure of a 9-5 workplace. The chaplain's 'On-Call' pager is like a tiny electrical pulse which can go berserk at any time, day or night. That belt buzzer puts a very different tension on the chaplain's nighttime. I would not want it any other way; some of the most precious healthcare encounters occur in the early hours of the morning. A patient is agitated or restless, another is aggressive, it could be end-of-life care for someone or support for a newborn baby and her family. These are a few of the situations in which the 'On-Call' chaplain can be summoned by staff, family, or patient. My first call-out was to be present at A & E as the injured and family of the deceased arrived at the hospital following a motorway crash - it was 1:00 am.

The unity in such a diverse chaplaincy department was a credit to the team, and in particular the head of department, Chris Swift. By reputation, he was one of the leading healthcare chaplains in the country. He was the author the NHS Chaplaincy Guidelines published in 2015. His wisdom and gentle leadership, together with his tenacity in fighting for the right to spiritual care for all was inspirational.

Having been a curate at Stanley and then a vicar in Wakefield, it was a joy to be, postremus inter pares, the least among equals in this thriving team. As I relaxed into this new role, I was able to be myself, and with that came the pranks and quips that sometimes got me in deep water but generally spread a chuckle around the department.

It was probably not the best idea to pass a referral to our deputy head, Tony, to go and visit a lady in the urology department. Her name was Ida Longpea. His pointless trip raised merriment on the ward. He did not fall for the second visit to Ivan Itch at the dermatology centre.

I suffered the wrath of Anne, our secretary, on the 1st of April - she arrived to find her office cordoned off with 'Restricted Access' tape. I had acquired the tape from builders working nearby. Her entry to the office was supposedly forbidden. After giving the builders a telling-off, she discovered it was a prank. I never owned up to it, but there was no doubt who closed the entire row of south-facing offices on Gledhow Wing, Level 6. Michael, the Roman Catholic chaplain, refused to hear my confession later that day.

The context of these instances of humour was the camaraderie in the chaplaincy team. I quickly realised my colleagues had many coping strategies that enabled them to absorb some of the stress and trauma that they encountered hour by hour. The chaplain sees herself as a confidential safety valve for others to let off steam or a safe haven to dump pain.

Holistic care is not only offered by the spiritual carers, staff contribute too, but when the chaplain 'loiters' on the ward, the intent is to be available for conversation and quiet reflection. When all around the patient can seem frantic and invasive the spiritual stranger offers time and space and allows the patient to set the agenda.

Not long after my appointment at Leeds, I was paged to visit Pam. She had just been given 'bad news' and was struggling to come to terms with her life-limiting diagnosis.

Pam was a 50-something mother of two adult boys and a granddaughter who was 'the love of her life.' The oncologist consultation when her bowel cancer was disclosed was shocking – hard for her to comprehend. She was active in personal fitness and lived a healthy lifestyle, and this 'news' had brought her to her knees - literally. The astute oncology ward sister asked her if she would like a visit from the chaplain.

Pam greeted me into the personal space of her bedside and was open about her cancer that was in the latter stages. She confessed that she felt like a hypocrite speaking to me because she had not 'bothered with God' up to now.

Several encounters followed, building up trust and spiritual companionship for this difficult journey in life. We spoke about bothering with God and how God longed to be a personal saviour and friend rather than a distant ogre. She tentatively took the booklet, 'Journey into Life' – Norman Warren - at the end of one of my visits.

The next day, Pam said she had read the booklet and would like to pray the prayer in the back of the book. As we prayed, curtains drawn, in the privacy of her bedside, tears lined her cheeks, 'I ask you, Lord Jesus, to come into my life as my Saviour… Lord… and friend, to be with me and within me. I will trust in you for the rest of my life.' I witnessed in my heart that Pam knew it to be true. God heard her prayer and held her tears. She was eternally secure - born again.

On the following visit, Pam said, it had been troubling her that she was not baptised. I spoke to the ward sister to see how we could achieve this new addition to her bucket list.

A few days later, the Baptism Service was held at St James's Hospital Chapel. The red-bricked Chapel dated back to 1861 and was unusual for its Romanesque arched windows framing a modest Rose window. Inside, Pam's family sat around the font in the domed basilica apse. I welcomed her mother, sister, two sons and granddaughter.

It was a joyous celebration, pregnant with poignancy because of her prognosis. Pam bowed her head over the font as I sprinkled her with water three times in the name of the Father, the Son, and the Holy Spirit. As the short, emotion-charged service drew to a close, Pam's son whispered in my ear, 'Would it be possible to baptise my daughter? I would love my mum to see her granddaughter baptised.'

Looking around the gathered party after I pronounced the sacramental words over the child, everyone's eyes were moist to overflowing, but Pam's sister seemed to be troubled. Afterwards, she said that she had felt convicted during the service that she had not made a personal commitment to Christ. A simple child-like prayer followed, and I duly reconvened the family gathering to witness Pam's sister's baptism.

Having been off the ward for some time, Pam was wilting, and a nurse ushered her back to the ward. She had received a triple blessing, and her family would never be the same again.

Several follow-up visits ensued, initially at Pam's home in Rothwell and towards the end of her earthly life in St Gemma's Hospice, where she passed peacefully from time into eternity.

There is much joy and sadness in healthcare chaplaincy, privilege, and poignancy. Pamela's story was one example of a chaplain being drawn into a person's narrative. These are brief encounters in the big picture of a life's journey. Nonetheless, they are deep and close encounters for the duration of that person's trauma.

One of my great pleasures at Leeds Teaching Hospitals (LTH) was in meeting and engaging with the staff. Some of these colleagues gave me a wide berth; their lack of faith was projected into their work environment. In these cases, the chaplain was a 'waste of space and resources.' I came alongside them, knowing it would be a long, slow journey of building up a trusting relationship. Others would greet me and admit that they had no faith, but they could appreciate the value that spiritual care added to the patient's experience of holistic care. I loved mixing and mingling with our staff teams. As chaplains, we consider ourselves to be one discipline among the multi-disciplinary teams (MDT) of hospital care.

At Leeds, I ended up on the 'Dignity in Care' team, the Palliative Care team, Credo - a research team, CareNet - a staff communications website together with some individual ward teams. After a while, I headed up Spiritual Care in Bexley - the new Leeds Cancer Centre.

All of these groups brought me shoulder to shoulder with staff colleagues, and many special friendships grew out of these meetings. Sometimes, staff would 'own up' to being Christians, and I tuned the radar of my prayer life and spiritual care towards them.

Jeanette was the lead sister at Wharfedale's Day Centre, which I visited every Friday morning. Her warmth towards Chaplaincy helped me forge important conversations with day patients. At noon, some of us would break from the mild hubbub of the centre and head for the 'treatment room,' where we would share Holy Communion, read scripture and pray. This was the only church service that most of them would participate in each week. The reverence, silently expressed, by each and every day-centre-worshipper was a lesson in awe and wonder that the church would do well to replicate.

After a few months of settling in, Jeanette called me into her office. In her Scottish brogue, she said, 'De ye ken that I am a Christian, Kelvin?'

'I thought you might be,' I responded, 'why didn't you say so before?'

'Ah well, I was' ne sure whether you would be a Christian yourself.' I pointed to my dog collar as if to self-justify.

'That wee bit of plastic means nothing, but I can see that the way you behave with these dear souls, that you truly are born again.'

Jeanette was a dour Scot who moved south from Ayrshire to follow her own vocation in Yorkshire. I would not have been surprised if she had been in the army before her calling. She ran a regimented day centre; no prisoners were taken, but patient-centred care was at the heart of it all.

She attended a Free-church in Otley and had no preconceived ideas that a 'chaplain,' by definition, would mean Christian - and she was right.

Over the years that followed, we became good friends, Christian brother and sister. She would speak at chaplaincy training days - giving a ward sister's perspective of holistic care - she was a gem in the staff team at Wharfedale.

Friday was my 'out and about' day. I joined the LTH Chaplaincy team for morning prayers at 8:30 am and then headed off through Harehills, Alwoodley and Bramhope and on to Wharfedale on the verge of the Yorkshire Dales. Those twelve miles - listening to sermons and worship music whilst drinking in the beautiful vista was my Friday delight. I lunched in the state-of-the-art hospital restaurant before heading back to Chapel Allerton Hospital and onto Seacroft Hospital. These satellite hospitals of Leeds were well supported by the chaplaincy team, and I got to go there every week; it was deep joy.

I often thanked the Lord for blessing me with this change in direction from parish ministry.

> I've been to Wharfdale and Seacroft and enjoyed my day. I was singing and praying in the spirit as I drove over the dales to Otley - gorgeous views of picturesque landscapes - life is good. Thank you, Lord.
>
> —Friday the 8th of February 2008

Each week, I looked forward to seeing doctor 'T.A.' at Seacroft. He was the senior 'junior' doctor on the Elderly Medicine wards. The first time I met him, he asked if we could share the sacrament of Holy Communion in the Chapel during his break.

T.A. was passionate about using his skills and knowledge in medicine to do God's healing work. He was a gentle, patient soul who testified that he had come to faith in St James'

Hospital Chapel. Sat alone as the sun's rays split through the Rose window, he heard an audible voice beckoning him to follow Jesus Christ. That encounter transformed his life, and as we worked together on the wards, he would often refer patients and staff to 'have a word' with the chaplain. It was a good working relationship of a couple of disciples and two disciplines coming together.

Dotted all over the sizeable Leads Teaching Hospital staff were Christian brothers and sisters, and I relished opportunities to engage and encourage them to live out their Christian faith in the workplace. A few of the Saint James' staff formed a prayer group: Tim, Nigel, Clara, Joy, Mel, Andrew, and others were a vital part of not only my Chaplaincy but also my Christian fellowship in the hospital. They were from different denominations and traditions of church, but we met to share and care for each other. We encouraged and bore one another's burdens as we stepped back from the cut and thrust of our different departments and then return strengthened by the koinonia, to 'shine like stars' in the workplace (Philippians 2:15).

Obviously, I was not just chaplain to staff who had my faith but to all faiths and those of none. One of the strangest call-outs I received in the line of duty was to 'tackle' a poltergeist that was manifesting itself in the staff creche and malingering in the corridors at night.

As I had a bit of experience with such phenomena in the parish at St Andrew's, Chris Swift suggested that I 'pay a visit'. I was under strict instructions to maintain confidentiality, be covert, and advise our staff not to 'gossip' about the details of the apparition beyond those who had first-hand experience. The press would have loved to sensationalise such matters, and our department's approach was to treat the staff's concern with the utmost seriousness and care.

I visited the creche and sat patiently by a bright button-patterned tablecloth with surrounding storage baskets of yellow and green. One by one, several nursery staff recounted their experience of the 'ghost.' Their recollections were surprisingly similar: 'a middle-aged lady in a long dark dress,' 'an unusual sensation of cold,' 'children just months old staring at something unseen.'

I wrote copious notes, reassuring staff that we were there to listen and record the testimonies and that we were in earnest about their supernatural revelations. I mentioned that, as a Christian chaplain, I believed prayer would have a significant effect on the matter. Staff were relieved that someone in our NHS Trust was prepared to hear their story and take them seriously.

Meeting with Dr TA on the wards after, I asked if he ever had a paranormal experience on the ward.

'Oh Yea,' he said, 'There is a lady in a long black dress that wanders the corridors some nights.'

He was most casual as he related his experiences that substantiated the creche staff accounts.

So, what to do? I discussed this with Dr Chris Swift after a few visits to the unit. No one was unduly distressed. Some of the staff placed significance on the fact that the old mortuary was just 50 metres from the new creche unit. I asked our head of department if I could go and pray in each location - instructing the presence to depart and cease from troubling staff, patients, and children – 'in the name of Jesus.' I was confident that this 'presence' would depart.

My boss looked at me as if I had just sprouted pointy ears and recoloured to green. 'Well, okay, if you wish, but take another chaplain with you - we don't do these things solo.'

The two Ghostbusters arrived at the creche after closing time. Armed with a couple of sachets of sterilised water and a kidney dish we walked from room to room and then to the corridors and prayed, sprinkled and trusted. There was nothing spectacular about the procedure or the response. But how powerful the name of Jesus is. There were no further reports of paranormal activity. This is just one of the bizarre situations a healthcare chaplain could get called into.

Most of my chaplaincy encounters came about by generically visiting certain wards on certain days with Fridays set aside for excursions further afield. I would arrive on a ward, a little apprehensive, and make contact with the charge nurse to inquire if there were any developments I needed to know about. Then it was onto the ward and see what happens when I introduced myself as 'the chaplain.' I believe the prayer at base before we went onto the wards was a vital bedrock before these visits.

On the 8th of January 2009, I met Steve, a patient in the Bexley wing of the Leeds Cancer Centre. After the, 'I'm the chaplain' and 'I'm not religious,' introductions were out of the way I asked Steve what sort of a day he was having. It was a good opening question that allowed Steve to be as open or closed as he wished.

'Not great,' he replied, 'I have a number of tumours on or around my liver, and they may be inoperable.'

'How do you deal with that sort of prognosis, Steve?'

'You have no choice,' he said as he sat up in his bed. 'Do you have a faith that you can turn to?' I ventured. 'Not really, listen,

I'm just getting what I deserve.'

'Really, what do you mean?'

'Well, the life I have lived of drink and drugs and rock'n'roll - this is how it ends up, and I guess I can have no complaints.'

I spoke to Steve about God, who can be his 'ever-present help' in his time of trouble. I sensed that he was open to a different way despite his concept of being left to suffer the consequences of a life of excesses. His 'que sera, sera' philosophy had nothing to offer as his tumours played Russian roulette with his insides. Steve warmed to the good news that there was a saviour called Jesus. With child-like simplicity, he turned away from his stoic self-resilience and handed his life over to the one who is eternally trustworthy.

After his discharge from Bexley, he turned up at St Helen's Church, Sandal. Jennie and our three girls had made this our place of worship after we left St Andrew's. I was welcomed by the vicar, Rev Rupert Martin and was pleased to support him when I was not doing the crazy Sunday hospital dash in Leeds. Three services in three different locations plus the demands of on-call and bedside Holy Communions.

Steve sat beside me in the nave at St Helen's. Our dark oak pew was framed by five pairs of stone columns supporting ogival arches and lofty vaulted ceilings beyond. We looked towards the gold cross mounted high on a glass wall at the rear of the dais.

As the service drew to a close, the minister invited those who required prayer for healing to move to a quiet area at the back of the church. My pew-mate, Steve, arose and walked gingerly to the narthex. In chaplain mode, I followed, and we sat together under a thousand years of intercessory history in the presence of a Holy God. As we prayed, I cannot explain what happened next. In truth, the prayer was nondescript, a prayer for healing, amen, and I asked Steve if he sensed that the Holy Spirit was with us. I am not sure that I did! Steve looked at me with tears in his eyes and calmly stated – 'I've been healed.'

'That's great,' I tentatively replied, 'did you feel the Lord's healing touch?'

'No, just these words spoken to me, 'You've been healed."

Oh, me of little faith, I thought, what does 'healing' mean? Was it a healing of peace amidst the turmoil of cancer? Was it contentment that he had faith to walk with God through this valley of the shadow of death? Surely, he could not mean a tumour-zapping miracle to confound the medics. But, yes, it was. I could only go along with his God-given assurance. It was not a gung-ho reckless confidence but a quietness and trust that was his strength (Isaiah 30:15).

Providentially, one of the nurses who worked at the Leeds Teaching Hospitals also attended the St Helen's service. Steve chatted with Joss over a coffee afterwards. That conversation led to a romance and a proposal. On the 20th November 2010 I stood in the sanctuary at St Helen's and my mind drifted back to that first meeting in Bexley. It was such a privilege to speak at Joss and Steve's wedding. Steve Thorndike is still well and good fourteen years later. God is very good.

Standing to preach, perched on full-length orthotics, leaning on crutches was becoming less practical as a healthcare chaplain. I still maintained upper body strength by standing and walking daily, but the distances I had to travel in the Leeds NHS Trust were so great that I had to adopt a common-sense approach and use a wheelchair. I gained a dubious reputation for dashing about in an 'Ultra-lightweight Quickie.'

Unlike historic church buildings, hospitals are great for accessibility: smooth floors, disabled 'rest-rooms,' lifts to each floor and secret corridors to access outer reaches of the Trust's estate. The NHS 'gets' equality in a way that the established church is lacking. The wheelchair is not objectified, and ableist language and metaphors are frowned upon.

I could sprint from the Chapel to Beckett Wing via an underground tunnel in less than five minutes. The wheelchair dash was all right until you met a porter transporting a patient in the opposite direction. Hospital porters were not happy about my speeding. I got my comeuppance heading down the hill on the tarmac to Gledhow Wing. Travelling at speed, I snagged a small stone on the front castors. Wipe-out, head over heels, I left the chair at an upward trajectory and came to a sit-still at the curb with the Quickie still in motion. Staff and visitors came to the rescue, and all that was bruised was my pride. All the fun of the fair at LTH.

In more ways than one, the time at Leeds flew by. Coming towards the end of my Masters in Theology (M.Th.), our lead chaplain, Chris Swift, in my annual review, recognised that I had leadership qualities that could transfer to other NHS trusts, but he said that he wanted me to stick around and be a part of the Leeds team for the long term.

I confessed to my boss that I had met with the lead chaplain of the Isle of Wight NHS Trust, Rev Dr Gregory Clifton-Smith and that I was praying for an opportunity to move to our favoured chalk-cliffed island off the Hampshire coast. Chris was so gracious as I broke the news to him. Nevertheless, from that point, the writing was on the wall. The move would take a further nine months, but the wheels were in motion.

FIFTEEN

Rita

I drove to Northern Ireland with my family to tell Mum about our move to the Isle of Wight. I was excited that I would be ministering as a healthcare chaplain and that my disability would not be an issue.

Rita Burke never really came to terms with my disability. It seemed to be an affront to her calling to 'minister to the sick.' The challenge was not, 'healer heal thyself' but 'healer heal thy son.' Not that Rita would ever have accepted the label 'healer.' She would say, 'Jesus is the only healer.'

The sadness in my mother's eyes may only have been apparent to me, but our relationship changed dramatically on the 30th of May 1979. From that day, I was in need of a miracle of healing, and it was her mission to pray without ceasing to accomplish that realignment and reconnection of my severed spinal cord. There was no point in mentioning the fact that my eleventh-thoracic vertebra was so crushed that there was no opening for the sheath of the spinal cord to reconnect or regenerate. Mum would simply assert that 'the Lord will do it, stop looking at the problem and look unto Jesus.'

Rita Burke was a glamorous, slender colleen with long, dark, shoulder-length locks. She was in her prime at 38 when she foolishly decided to go for a ride on one of our horses, Rusty, who stood sixteen hands at his withers. She saddled up and climbed on in the paddock adjacent to our home in Cornascriebe. It was the summer of 1965, and the going was good for Billy and Rita Burke and their three boys. The youngest, Richard was just 18 months old.

Moments after mounting the stead, Mum attempted a show jump on the dark-maned chestnut. She was thrown to the ground, landing head first. At nine years of age, I stood on a windowsill in our home, staring in disbelief as the ambulance came to rush her to hospital. Her neck was broken at the sixth cervical vertebrae, and her right arm had multiple fractures from the fall.

Rita Burke's testimony of the episode is that she fervently prayed to the Lord in that Lurgan hospital and vowed that if Jesus would miraculously heal her and restore her to tend and care for her young family, she would offer her life in service to 'praying for the sick.'

On her third day in hospital, my mother believed in her heart that she was 'every whit whole' and told the medics caring for her that she wanted to convalesce at home with 'her boys.' To the disapproval of the staff, Rita discharged herself three days after admission, having suffered a broken neck and a smashed arm - healed and restored.

At the age of 83, the years transposed, she telephoned me on the 30th of May 2010 to say, prophetically, that I would be healed that very day. She was oblivious that it was the anniversary of my Honister accident. After thirty-one years of being a paraplegic, I had grown used to being an emotional pin cushion for 'words' like these.

> My mother has just phoned me at 7:30 pm and said, 'You are healed. If you have faith to believe it, you will be healed today.' It's hard to know how to react - Mum doesn't know it is the anniversary of my accident – thirty-one years and how I would dearly love to be healed and to receive it physically today. I feel like an emotional pin cushion to anyone who wants to experiment faith on me.
>
> —Sunday the 30th May 2010

I would often find myself a target for well-meaning people who felt led to pray for me. I had developed hide as thick as a rhinoceros towards strangers who violated me in Christian gatherings. But this was my mother, and her desperation to see her son walk again grew stronger as her own health deteriorated. Jennie and I often prayed that the Lord would work a wonder so that my mother could witness my physical healing before she died.

Wishing to tell Mum about our move to the Isle of Wight, I longed for an understanding with her that the Lord had placed her son in the sphere of healthcare, not despite the disability but including it and using it in His service and for His glory.

Despite the Giff Claiborne prophecy, Rita never got the irony of her middle son being involved in the healing ministry. In truth, she never really appreciated the whole 'calling' thing at all. She was present at my ordination in Wakefield Cathedral in 1999, and she knew about the transition to whole-time hospital chaplaincy in 2006, but I was still her wee boy who was paralysed in a car crash in 1979. At the right time, the Lord Jesus would say to me, 'Rise up and walk,' and she longed for that day.

I sat alongside this octogenarian in her Parker Knoll recliner and gave her a large print Gideon Bible. We opened it to read a Bible passage together. It fell open at Mark's Gospel, Chapter One, the prologue, 'The beginning of the Good News about Jesus.'

In a childlike manner, Rita interrupted, 'He is still the good news, isn't he?'

'Amen,' I retorted.

'Is that what you tell the people in hospital?'

'Yes, if I get an opportunity, I can't ram it down people's throats, Mum.'

'No, but Jesus will minister to people in the hospital through you.'

'I hope so.'

'That's why he wants you to go to the Isle of Wight.'

I was dumbfounded, not that she had mentioned the big move, I had spoken on the telephone to her about that; I finally realised that, despite her obsession with my accident, she knew, deep down, that God would use it for his glory. Just as he had used her riding accident to bring about a lifelong commitment to 'praying for the sick.'

We continued our reading in Mark, 'The baptism of Christ,' delivered another surprise.

'I have been waking in the night, troubled that I have never been baptised in water. I know I am baptised in the Holy Spirit but not with water.'

She looked at me with trepidation in her eyes and asked,

'Will you Baptise me in water, Kelvin?'

You could have knocked me down with a feather. This was more than a plea for a dunking - this was recognition that I was a minister. The disability was invisible in this request. She saw me as a servant of the Lord who could say 'yea' or 'nay' to her fearful request.

As if I would say no, 'Of course,' I said.

My mind was already working out the logistics of a Rev in a wheelchair and an 83-year-old female both waist-deep in water.

It was a bright Sabbath morn; the sun's rays pierced Venetian blinds as we gathered around the baptistery. The congregation was small; Jennie, our three girls, and my brother Richard turned up to witness. As formal as a gathering in a bathroom could be, I asked the candidate clad in Whitsunday garb,

'Do you repent of the sin that separates us from God?'

'Do you submit to Christ as Saviour and Lord?'

'Do you come to Christ, the way, the truth and the life?'

To these questions, the eighty-three-year-old replied in turn, 'I repent, I submit, I come to Christ.'

Jennie helped me submerge my mother backwards into the tepid water in the name of the Father, the Son and the Holy Spirit. As Rita sat forward, joy filled her well-drenched face as we embraced. The sadness in her eyes was gone, not that her son was healed but because she allowed thirty-one years of hurt to be washed away that day.

We flew from Belfast airport that afternoon. It had been a special visit for me, it would not be long before we would be packing our bags again to immigrate to that little caulkhead commune off the Hampshire coast.

The day of our move, the 4th of September 2010, was one crazy day.

Jennie said, 'Only you would be so stupid to book a self-drive van and agree to lead and preach at two Sunday Services on the day we leave!'

That is exactly how it was. We were cramming twenty-four years of post-wedding furniture, books and stuff into a 7.5-tonne Box Van until darkness filled the early hours of the Sabbath. David Popple set off for the Island at 3.45 am and we managed a few hours snooze before I clocked in at St Helen's Parish Church for the 9.15 am Morning Service.

Jennie arrived with the three girls, Charlie, our King Charles Spaniel and Sam, the turtle just in time for the 10.45 am Eucharist.

A prayer scrum send-off concluded the Sunday Service, and the Burkes were on the M1 at 1 pm heading, 'like lilty' for the 5 pm Ferry from Portsmouth to Fishbourne.

There were cards, balloons, and banners, plus a food hamper to welcome us to 'Cornerways,' our new home in Ventnor. The panoramic sea views beyond the great Cedars of the Botanic Gardens would be our new outlook.

That crazy day ended with a dark starry sky and a waning crescent moon casting a faint reflection on the English Channel. Jennie and I embraced and thanked our creator God for this new chapter in our lives. In that stillness, Deuteronomy 31:8 resonated with the cicada's call, 'It is the Lord who goes before you. He will be with you, he will not leave you or forsake you. Do not fear or the dismayed.'

SIXTEEN

All this Beauty

As I drove in to register as an honorary Chaplin in 2010, St. Mary's Hospital in Newport resembled a steel-clad army of Japanese samurai. It had opened just twenty-one years earlier and was, back then, heralded as a pioneering low-energy hospital. The light grey cladding and Koan sculpture depict a brightness that permeates the mood in the corridors and wards within.

The Chaplaincy Department was strategically sited at one of the busiest thoroughfares of the hospital. It is one of the smallest departments in the Trust and comprised of a Christian Chapel, a Multi-faith quiet room and an office. Our team of four paid chaplains was enhanced by a swell of goodwill and energy that flowed from honorary chaplains and chaplaincy volunteers.

It enabled us to punch above our weight as a spiritual presence in the Isle of Wight NHS Trust.

Initially, I was employed to provide chaplaincy support at

Mountbatten Hospice. It suited me down to the ground, I was back on the road, just like my Fridays at Leeds. I would be flitting between St. Mary's Hospital and the Hospice three days per week as stipulated in the 'Service Level Agreement.'

Mountbatten was a thriving eighteen-bed Hospice with a Day Care facility - the JCC, John Cheverton Centre, that was a flagship of excellent care provided to people on the Island with life-limiting illness.

Three mornings per week, I would routinely visit every person in the ensuite rooms and the JCC, who were open to a greeting from the chaplain. Chaplaincy volunteers complemented this pattern to provide a prayerful presence every working day of the week. Once a month, we held a Holy Communion service in the Chapel. A smattering of visitors, patients, volunteers and staff would join in this reflective sacramental service. It was a blessed pause amidst the holistic traffic of the Hospice.

I first met Sandi on my JCC rounds. She was a bit of a bookworm and cradled her latest read intensely as I introduced myself as 'the new chaplain.' She lowered her book sufficiently to tell me her parents were 'C of E' and added, 'I haven't really kept the faith.' Fair enough, Sandi had laid down the parameters that our encounters would continue within over the weeks and months ahead.

Sandi was a young single mum, anxious about what would happen to her children 'if anything happened' to her. Her son was a year older, and her daughter was a year younger than Ellie, my youngest daughter (age 14). I could understand her angst. Over subsequent visits, she would open up some more about her desire that her parents would care for her two children and not her 'ex' after her inevitable passing.

One morning, I answered a knock on my office door and

was surprised to see Sandi standing, wanting to come in and close the door to talk privately. 'Could I come to the monthly communion service?' she asked sheepishly.

'Of course, you would be most welcome.'

'I have been thinking about my faith again. I prefer not to speak in front of all the people in the JCC.'

'I can understand that, you can talk in confidence here.'

Tears welled up as her eyes stared at the floor, and she asked, 'When I am dying, how will I know and what do I do?'

Wow, that's a question and a half, I thought. It is a query of a person wanting to be ready to meet her maker. I fired a prayer heavenward for wisdom and sensitivity to this blessed daughter's aching heart.

'I thought that I was dying once,' I replied. 'It was after my car accident; I was conscious, my eyes were open, but the world was in darkness. I felt permanently winded and was living on quarter breaths. In that desperate state, the name 'Jesus' came into my head, not as a swearword but a prayer.'

Sandi listened intently as I continued, 'I kept repeating his name over and over in my head, an unspoken one-word prayer - Jesus - to the rhythm of my racing heartbeat.'

I shared a Bible verse with her, a verse I discovered months later, 'His name is like ointment poured forth,' Song of Solomon 1:3.

It was more than a year later when nurse Sarah paged me to say Sandi was nearing the end of her life. I went to her room in the Hospice without delay, knocked and entered. Her two children were sat at mum's bedside. Sandi's mother was also there comforting both daughter and grandchildren. It felt like I was intruding as I asked if I could say a prayer with her.

I wheeled closer and bowed my head in silent prayer. Her breathing was irregular and strained, yet her demeanour was serene. I sought wise words to say, but none were forthcoming; it felt awkward - I was awkward. At that moment, Sandi's weak whisper broke the silence; she spoke His name, 'Jesus,' softly and tenderly. This was no swear word; it was a reaching out to her Lord, strength and shield, ever-present help. She spoke it again and again like a pulse leading her peacefully on. I left her side, knowing she was safe and secure. Later that morning, Sandi journeyed through the valley of the shadow of death to be with her Lord – Jesus is his name.

There were a few deaths of 'young ones' that week. It took its toll on the nursing staff. Some of them would sit reflecting in the Chapel, others would knock on my door and say, 'Can I have a word?' Those were precious exchanges between the chaplain and nursing colleagues. They may have 'why?' questions or express emotional empathy or distress that requires a time-out to try and process the impact those young lives lost were having on them. It was a privilege to be a trusted listener and intercessor in these encounters.

The drive across Newport to St Mary's Hospital enabled a physical disconnect with some of the painful and difficult visits that had transpired that morning. I 'clocked-in' at the office; volunteers Ian and Stella were just departing after their morning on the wards. The Roman Catholic Eucharistic ministers were just arriving for their cohort. Janet Hallam, Deputy-lead Chaplain, was posting her notes onto the system. After pleasantries, I entered the Chapel alone and sat motionless, hands upward, eyes scanning the golden text etched on the sanctuary wall, 'The Spirit of God descending like a dove and alighting on him.' I shed a tear for Sandi and her children and her mother and the staff who had been blessed by knowing her. It was my first tears of the day as I grieved at losing her. I hoped with all my heart that the voice from heaven at Christ's Baptism - as recorded on the Chapel wall - could extend to me, 'This is my son whom I love, with him I am well pleased.'

The Chapel at St. Mary's was a great sanctuary for the hospital. Staff, visitors, patients, and chaplains alike found solace in this safe and holy space. I felt strengthened after morning prayers with my chaplain colleagues at the start of each day as we committed ourselves afresh for the day and its tasks.

Before I met her in person, Gina was a name in the hospital prayer requests book dated 8th August 2012.

'Please pray for my darling daughter Gina. Signed: Sue'

We prayed for Gina as a chaplaincy team, and within minutes of wheeling along the first-floor corridor, Doctor Randall stopped me and asked if I could give support to a patient called 'Gina.' She had a Christian faith and was praying for a miracle, but 'she is gravely ill,' he said.

'Gina was a community nurse who had a late diagnosis of stage four cancer,' the doctor continued.

Gina and her husband, Chris, were active members of the 'Church on the Roundabout.' Before I could get to visit her, she had been transferred to the Hospice. The following day, I sat poised in the Thursday morning Multi-disciplinary Team Meeting (MDT) at Mountbatten Hospice. At the mention of a new admission, Gina, I unclasped my hands from behind my head and leaned forward. 'We are concerned about this patient. She is in denial about the seriousness of her condition,' the presenter continued, 'Gina is extremely weak with a distended abdomen; she believes she will be miraculously healed.'

I sensed the Lord's nudge and whisper, 'She needs an ally,' and I spoke up, 'This lady is not in denial; it is her faith to believe and not doubt.'

'But she is deteriorating rapidly, in some pain and resisting pain relief.'

'Let me visit Gina to offer support,' I countered.

'Sounds like a good plan,' agreed Ian, the palliative consultant.

I knocked on Gina's door and was invited to enter. Her long brown hair hung limp around concave cheeks, but her smile was broad and welcoming. I drew alongside her bed and introduced myself.

I held her shrivelled skin and bone hand and said, 'The Lord tells me you need an ally.'

Gina laughed and asked, 'Why would that be?'

'Our nurses are worried about you, suffering unduly and holding out for a miracle.'

'Yes, I am. The Lord has healed me before, and he will do it again.'

I asked if she had a Bible verse that inspired her. Gina said without hesitation, James 1:6, 'When you ask, you must believe and not doubt.'

'I thought it might be that,' I said.

She peered at me purposefully, weighing me up - was I liberal or evangelical, was I a Charismatic or not?

'Praise God,' I said in agreement.

'So, don't be giving me negative vibes,' she added with a smile.

'I am here to support you; I have said to our staff that this is your faith, and we must respect that.'

'Thank you.'

We spoke about Raphael, the love of her life, just two years old, and her longing to see him grow up. I could feel this mother's love for an infant she wanted so desperately to nurture to adulthood.

'Who is helping with Raphael while you are in the Hospice?' I asked.

'His aunt Louise, my sister, she has been great, treats him like one of her own, she has three boys.'

I met Gina daily from that Thursday encounter. She was determined to build up her strength with fortified drinks. She was preparing for a theatre procedure that would reduce the swelling in her abdomen. We ended each visit with prayer for healing, a miracle that would baffle the medics.

Gina attended the monthly Eucharist in the Hospice Chapel on 13th August 2012. It was a simple service on the 10th Monday after Trinity Sunday. The Gospel reading from John 6, Jesus said 'I am the bread of life whoever comes to me will never be hungry whoever believes in me will never be thirsty - and I will raise them up on the last day.'

After reading the word, I took bread and broke it demonstratively, then held up the chalice and gave thanks. I wheeled around the seven believers sharing, 'the body and blood of Christ.' Gina received with her brothers and sisters in that Chapel, her cheeks wet with tears and glowing with adoration for her Lord Jesus.

Her door was ajar when I called the following day. She motioned for me to enter and close the door.

'Do you think I am crazy believing for a miracle?'

'No, I understand your trust in the Lord, and he is able to do it.'

I ventured, 'I do have a concern, however, Gina, with determination like yours, you may be closing down some tender moments you could be having with your family.'

I explained to her that it would not be regarded as doubt if she expressed gratitude to Sue, her mother, who had guided her to faith in her teens, or to Louise, for her care and support over the years and especially now. 'You could even write a letter to Raphael that he would treasure one day when he is able to comprehend how much you love him and all that you have gone through.' We prayed and parted for another day.

Gina's smile was wider than her face the morning after as she said, 'I did what you said. Wrote letters and wept buckets as I wrote some stuff I wish I had said before. I've even recorded a song for Rapha, one I have been singing to him. I even spoke to Louise and Aiden to ask them to be Raphael's guardians, if things went pear shaped.'

Gina seemed liberated, a burden lifted, no more striving to believe and not doubt. She gained a freedom to trust and hold on to the Lord who would surely 'raise her up on the last day' - whenever that may be. I gave her a 'holding cross' crafted from olive wood in a workshop in Bethlehem. 'Use this like a tactile prayer, 'Lord, I am holding onto you."

On Monday, 21st July 2012, with her girth widening and her strength waning, Gina crossed Newport by ambulance from the Hospice to the theatre at St. Mary's for the stents that she desperately needed. Her song for the journey was Matt Redman's: '10,000 Reasons.' Sue met her at St Mary's after scribbling another prayer in the chaplaincy prayer book. They sang together:

'The sun comes up, it's a new day dawning, it's time to sing your song again. Whatever may pass and whatever lies before me. Let me be singing when the evening comes.'

Their total confidence and trust was in the Lord Jesus.

Gina died in theatre, she was singing, 'when the evening comes,' in her heavenly home where she received her healing and her resurrection life.

A chaplain may visit seventy-five people per week, but each encounter touches you and humbles you in some way. In a few of those, a bond is forged and when it 'goes pear-shaped' it breaks you and tears fall.

I was a stranger to Gina's family, but I wept at her passing, not denying the glory that awaits her but for those who are left and in a strange way, it bothered me that we did not rustle up a miracle of healing this side of Jordan.

Sue Leeson continued to post prayer requests in the Chapel prayer book on a regular basis - for friends and neighbours who were ill and in need of a miracle.

Ten years later, in 2022, I finally met Louise. I was preaching at St. Andrews, Chale. Her 12-year-old son was by her side, his name is Raphael. Louise said fondly, 'He has two mums, Mummy Gina, and Mummy Louise - that is how we deal with it.'

I reached into the back of my wheelchair and grasped the holding cross that I believe the Lord prompted me to bring to church that morning. It was for Raphael. As I gave it to him, I said, 'This is exactly like the cross I gave your Mummy Gina the last time I prayed with her.'

The Sunday service in St Mary's Hospital Chapel was a vibrant time of worship. The congregation was gathered from those well enough to leave the wards and half a dozen volunteers who gave up their Sunday morning to make it happen. I was blessed by the generosity and commitment of the chaplaincy volunteers who would fetch and return patients to and from the wards. That brief encounter from ward to Chapel often forged a fellowship that prepared the way for the Eucharist that followed. Jennie would 'tinkle the ivories' in hearty worship, and a short preach on the word and breaking the bread had a transformative effect on many who attended. Some erstwhile patients continue to join our Sunday worship post-discharge. They had found faith or grown in faith through a spiritual awakening as inpatients.

Helen was discharged from the hospital to a Care Home in Cowes after a prolonged period of illness. She was so determined to continue in fellowship at St Mary's that she arranged for Paul, her carer, to drop her off at the Chapel each Sunday and collect her afterwards. She attended for several years before her health deteriorated further, and I was privileged to sit with this blessed sister, holding her hand at 9:30 am as she was promoted to worshipping her Saviour face to face on 18th July 2017.

Patients often speak with gratitude about their spiritual journeys alongside the chaplain at a time of great vulnerability and uncertainty. When the givens in life are stripped away, like health and independence, mobility - walking and driving, possessions - house and savings, friends and family, it is then that the message of 'what a friend we have in Jesus,' who draws near to comfort and rescue the lost - is so powerful. I witnessed it many times, and sometimes, I got to share it with their loved ones at their funeral, as I did for Helen Ives on 2nd August 2017.

One of the surprises I found as a Lead Chaplain was the number of civic occasions that there were. I would be called on to take the lead for the hospital. The Armistice Day remembrance or the opening of a dementia garden are two examples. The Lights of Love Memorial service at Newport Minster for the Hospice was another. This service was an annual pilgrimage for many families who had lost loved ones through life-limiting illness. The annual Children's Memorial service in June was another chaplaincy-led service for friends and family to remember children who had died.

There was a moment before each of these occasions where I would pause and glance around the gathered and pray for ambassadorial presence and personality to engage with each and every person desiring a fresh spiritual encounter with God in remembrance of loved ones.

St. Paul reminded Christians at Corinth that we are ambassadors for Christ, as though God was appealing to others through us, 'be reconciled to God,' (2 Corinthians 5:20). That is the responsibility I felt in those civic services where the majority of the congregation were unchurched people. At the conclusion of the meeting, invariably, people would approach me, teary-eyed or smiling - wishing to express their gratitude for the leading or preaching. Some wished to make further inquiries about coming to faith, others wanted to express their sensing of the otherness and mystery of God in that place, and a few more simply wanted to tell me their story of a loved one who had died. I felt honoured to be entrusted with this feedback and would often remind myself that the glory and the pre-eminence was for Christ alone (Colossians 1:18).

It was not these public situations that energised me, it was the fifteen plus, daily encounters with patients, family and staff that enlivened me more than any other aspect of being a chaplain. The small acts of kindness at the bedside, like cleaning someone's spectacles, softly singing a hymn, giving a holding cross, or spoon-feeding a meal, were important ways in which we could share the love of Christ with others. None of the above would feature in a chaplain's job description but that role of a minister without portfolio in a healthcare setting suited me down to the ground.

The structure planned for the day would go out the window with a 'chance' meeting in the lift, being stopped by someone in the corridor, or checking in at the Chapel and finding a person in tears. I tried to emphasise to the chaplaincy team that ours is the 'ministry of interruptions.' Chaplains must be organised too, like everyone else in the NHS, but above all, we have to be available to God and to the beck-and-call of the NHS.

My best-laid plans for the evening on 21st February 2017 were aborted by a phone call from the ward sister on Colwell ward.

'One of the patients says he has to see you tonight.'

I asked if his health was deteriorating, was it an emergency, to which the nurse replied,

'No, he's fine but he's kicking off saying he needs to see the chaplain tonight - his name is Robin.'

'Okay, I will come right away.'

Robin had attended our Sunday service the previous day. He was a few days short of his thirty-second birthday. His neck and limbs were a canvas for an elaborate array of 'tats' that his NHS pyjamas failed to conceal.

As we spoke after the weekly service, he said, 'I am Gloria's son; you know Gloria from the Hospice; you did the funeral.'

'Yes, I remember Gloria - she called me 'Vicarage' after the 'Rev' sitcom. Gloria loved to wind me up about God and stuff.'

'Yeah, that's her - she thought the world of you.'

'That's nice, but I don't remember you from the funeral.'

'Nah, I was a mess, I couldn't make it.'

Robin began to tell me that his life had spiralled out of control with drug and alcohol dependency. I agreed to meet him on the ward the following morning when I could hear more of his story.

After morning prayers and a few emails, he was my first visit of the day. Robin's frame filled his bed on Colwell ward. His presence filled the whole curtained cubical – D6.

I rolled up alongside him and was greeted like a long-lost friend. We got into all sorts about his life story. He was a promising teenage rugby player in the Welsh schoolboys U16 team. He was into Heavy Metal music; Greenday, Metallica, and Fall Out Boy tripped off his tongue. Robin was proud to be a tattoo artist and had worked at the Black Rose studio in Cowes. He loved ComiCon and LARP, dressing up in mediaeval costumes and camping out around wood fires and eating spit-cooked food.

Robin had packed a lot into 32 years, but his excesses had

taken its toll on his liver. After a long discourse, I asked Robin what did he think that I, as a chaplain, could do for him.

His forehead frowned a pleading look, 'I need to know that what you said yesterday about Jesus was true.' I had preached on Luke 13 and these words of Jesus, 'as a hen gathers her brood under her wings... I desired to gather you,' had penetrated his soul.

'It is 100% true and far more besides, Robin. I sense that you have been trying to fill your life with things that cannot give lasting satisfaction.'

'Too right,' He replied.

'Someone [Blaise Pascal] once said that within every person is a God-shaped vacuum which only Jesus can fill. Your mother placed her life into the Lord's hands when we prayed together, and He is the answer you are looking for, Robin.'

'I need a Bible,' he blurted.

I gave him a Gideon Bible that I had in the back pouch of my wheelchair and turned it to page 3: 'Where to find help in times of need.'

Robin grasped the Good Book and said he would read it and let me know what he thought.

'Time grabs you by the wrist and directs you where to go.'

'What's that from?' I queried.

'Greenday – Time of your life.'

'Maybe, God 'grabs you by the wrist' is what is happening to you,' I retorted.

Robin smiled and gave a contented nod as we separated. I

assured him that I would schedule to visit him in a couple of days' time to see how he was doing. That was the plan, but my pager buzzed at 9:00 pm and the ward sister tells me that Robin needs to see me that night.

I hastily pulled on my uniform - clergy shirt and dog collar and was at his bedside by 9:30 pm. 'What is troubling you, Robin?' I ventured.

'Nothing. I have been reading this Bible all day, and I need to do this tonight?'

'Do what tonight?'

'The prayer that you helped my mother pray, to have Jesus in her life.'

I pulled the curtains around; I could see the visitors in D Bay becoming intrigued by this brazen, tattoo-clad young man engaging with the 'Vicarage.' Curtains could not sound proof our exchanges but they provided a confidential safe space where I could hold the hand of this seeking soul.

Our thumbs interlocked as I led him in a simple prayer that introduced him to my Lord and his Saviour - Jesus Christ. The two of us wept at the realisation that Robin had a new Lord - he was eternally secure. It would be a hard road ahead; the cravings for his counterfeit gods would continue to tempt, but he was now trusting in the one who could be his ever-present help in times of trouble.

Robin joined the AA group which met weekly in our chaplaincy multi-faith room, and I took him to, and introduced him to, a local church the Sunday following his discharge. These would give him ongoing support on that narrow road that leads to life (Matthew 7:14).

I left Colwell ward at 11 pm, glowing with joy as I drove home to Ventnor. The moonlight silhouetted thatched roofed cottages along the way. Whatever Monday evening could have been, I would not have missed witnessing Robin's name being etched in the 'Book of Life' for anything.

Chaplaincy encounters like Robin, Gina, Sandi and Helen were the kind of case studies that we brought to our regular team Reflective Practise sessions. I fervently believe that chaplains need to be frequent reflective practitioners, where the whole chaplaincy team meet to learn from our experiences, share pain and joys and identify changes that could influence future encounters for the better.

After all, I have kept a diary since I was a teenager. Journaling, writing down thoughts and prayers, and reflecting on parish happenings have been an important learning and developmental modus operandi for me over the years.

I first reflected on the powerful effect that Maths teacher Barbara Burgess had on a young student who subsequently suffered his own life-changing trauma. We grow and learn by taking time to reflect and pray. Prayer does not simply express needs and wants; prayer changes us. We cannot come into the presence of God without being changed. I find that, in my quiet times, I rest in the shadow of the cross where Christ's wounds and my reflections bring healing and sustenance.

Looking back, I reflect on God providentially directing Jennie to a tiny advert in the Church Times about Healthcare Chaplaincy at the very time that I was perched in the Hospital Chapel asking for guidance.

When I transferred to Healthcare Chaplaincy from the Church of England, I thought that my days as a preacher and evangelist had gone. Despite neither featuring in my job description, I preached over 300 times and saw more people come to faith in my years as a chaplain than in my time as a vicar.

Like the writer of Psalm 103, I can reflect on all the benefits and blessings of a lifelong journey with my Lord: redemption, healing, forgiveness, good things and a growing awareness of his faithful love and compassion. To date, I have not received the physical healing that I would dearly love, but day by day He satisfies and renews me, and He is all I need. In the words of St. Paul, 'I have learned to be content.'

There was one thing that I had to do before I felt closure on the 1979 accident that transported me from the ranks of the able-bodied to the disabled.

It was a dark winter's night as I parked up at the hospital. The snowfall was beginning to settle, and Jennie brought my wheelchair to the driver's door. I had been here once before, but today, 5th January 2020, I was filled with some trepidation as I entered the main reception.

The last time I was here, I read these words from Psalm 27 in my morning quiet time, 'I remain confident of this, I will see the goodness of the Lord in the land of the living. Wait for the Lord, be strong and take heart.' I leaned on these words once again as I buzzed the intercom of the Intensive Care Unit at West Cumberland Hospital, Whitehaven.

How can you express, over an intercom, that you just want to revisit a place where your life has been saved?

'It is Kelvin Burke, an ex-patient, I just want to say thank you.'

'Come in,' said the voice as the door was unlocked.

I rolled into the central hub and was greeted by the matron.

'I was a patient here for six days over forty years ago, and you kept me going through my darkest nights. I just wanted to come back and say thank you.'

'We are grateful for your appreciation.'

'Over the years, I have become a hospital chaplain and spent many hours visiting Intensive Care Units, holding hands and sharing the holistic care that you offer.'

She smiled and said, 'Thank you for saying thank you'.

In my mind, that was where this malarkey all began. That was the day this twenty-three-year-old eejit was pinned under a Morris Traveller car in that ravine off Honister Pass, blue-lighted to Whitehaven, lungs pierced and paralysed; it was the beginning of a journey I could never have imagined. And because of the trauma and the lengthy rehabilitation and the disability, there has been assumed empathy and rapport with those who received a visit from 'the chaplain in the wheelchair.'

Ever since I knelt as a ten-year-old to invite Jesus Christ into my life, the scriptures have nourished me, the Lord has guided me, and as he spoke on Honister, 'He has been with me always.'

I cannot say, in hindsight, like some Paralympians - I would do it all again. No, I wouldn't wish paralysis on anyone, but if it means I can be an ambassador for God or the finest way that he can be glorified in my life or to ensure that in all things he can have the pre-eminence then I would reply every time

– 'not my will but yours be done.'

EPILOGUE

Lake of Tears: Revisited

Reflecting, years later, on the Lake of Tears experience, what do I make of it?

Do I really think there is a lake 'up there' somewhere in the heavens? Does God have an actual record of our misery, held in a bottle, as depicted by the Psalmist?

As Johnny Mathis wrote, 'There are more questions than answers.'

No, I am not saying there is a literal lake of tears 'up there' but that's the vision that I received, and I have shared that with you in Chapter 9. We read in Isaiah 40:12 that God measures the oceans in the hollow of his hand. That's a picture of the greatness of God, beyond our comprehension and I believe that the Lake of Tears is a similar, staggering, glimpse that God is an all-knowing, all-participating ever-present God. Furthermore, and crucially so, that the tears that are recorded are ours and His.

Does the bible actually record that God cries with us? To be honest, I am not sure, I cannot give a clear-cut bible reference.

Yes, God can be grieved and God weeps and clearly Jesus, God incarnate, wept in anguish in Gethsemane, he wept with those who wept in John 11:35. Do we really believe, through the Apostle Paul, God would give a divine command (Romans 12:15b) such as 'weep with those who weep' if He was not active in that respect. I do not think so.

The record of the shortest verse in the bible, which sadly is more frequently used as a swearword, 'Jesus wept,' is a clear depiction of our Lord's lacrimony. There is some ambiguity about why Jesus wept at the time of Lazarus's death. After all, he had waited until his death was assured knowing he would reveal his personhood as the 'resurrection and the life.'

Some say he wept because he loved Lazarus. He was a frequent visitor to his home in Bethany. Others say he wept at Mary and Martha's and indeed the mourner's unbelief. I prefer the idea that he empathised with Mary and Martha's pain and that tears welled and dropped as he drew alongside them and others in their sadness. These were tears of compassion. This sits well with scriptures such as Psalm 147:3 and Psalm 34:18 which say He heals and is close to the broken-hearted. This depicts the empathetic nature of God.

In another instance, despite the joy and elation of Palm Sunday, 'Jesus wept' over Jerusalem because he foreknew the horrors that lay ahead of that city and because they did not recognise him as Messiah (Luke 19:41-44).

The Lord probably wept differently in these two situations because the eternal outcomes were entirely different. Martha, Mary, and Lazarus had eternal life because they believed in the Lord Jesus Christ, but the majority of the people of Jerusalem did not believe and therefore did not have life. I must have said this verse publicly at funerals and thanksgiving services some five hundred times - Jesus said… 'I am the resurrection and the life; he who believes in Me will live even if he dies' (John 11:25). This scripture sums up the eternal reality for those who believe Jesus, even if (and when) we die.

I need to revisit the verse I referenced in Chapter 9, Psalm 56:8: 'You keep track of all my sorrows. You have collected all my tears in your bottle. You have recorded each one in your book' NLT.

Remember David who wrote those words was a warrior. A Goliath slayer who had also fought off lions and bears in his shepherding days. Strange that he is admitting and emphasising tears. There should be no shame in tears. The most surprising statement is that not only does God keep a record, but he also holds our tears. I have come to realise that this is very significant.

David was under attack, mentally and physically, and he had made some poor decisions. He turned (actually, returned) to God. That was the most sensible thing he could have done. God not only knew of his tears, he held them and I believe the Lord wept with him. 'Weep with those who weep" is not simply a word from God it is a Word of God. It oozes compassion and pastoral care. That's what our Lord does. I suggest that God added tears to David's (more for the lake of tears)! Not one tear is wasted or ignored. Even your silent weeping, hidden sorrow, the Lord knows these situations. God is that close. Next time you weep - hear this, that he is close, alongside you, weeping with you, holding you catching your tears in his cupped-up hands. What a picture of God's love for us that is.

That was the Lord's answer to my arrogant rant, 'Lord, you don't know me, you don't see the tears I cry, you don't realise this is harder than I can bear.' He replied that every tear was noticed, caught, held, and added to by God who weeps with those who weep (Romans 12:15).

The Lake of Tears vision went on for over an hour (with me sobbing all the while). Time seemed to stand still, and I was broken by it. When I regained my composure, I realised God had spoken very clearly, it was emphatic, and I could not ignore it. God is ever-present, all-knowing, compassionate, and gentle. This is not about the Lord remembering or recording my misery and your hardship. This is God saying, he is Emmanuel, God with us, he will never leave us or forsake us – just as he spoke to me on Honister pass, he is with us always.

There is a caveat. When the bible refers to tears and weeping, it is not for wallowing in the misery of it but for the triumph and the Christ-like fragrance that exudes when we cling to God in his word and in prayer, in praise and in worship. 2 Corinthians 2:14 says 'he causes us to triumph and through us diffuses the fragrance of his knowledge in every place' NKJV. Imagine that underneath each of us is a little bottle of scent with those reed diffusers protruding. The aroma we exude would be beautiful. Throughout the bible brokenness and tears are the raw materials of flourishing and fruitfulness and the fragrance of Christ. Strange but so true in our lives too.

Psalm 126:5 'Those who sow in tears will reap with songs of joy. Those who go out weeping carrying seed to sow will return with songs of joy, carrying sheaves with them.' This is another metaphor, a picture given to us to glimpse a spiritual reality – a farming metaphor – sowing seeds and coming back with harvest.

This Psalm promises that, from our sowing in tears, a joyful harvest will be reaped provided we cling to God through his word and in prayer, praise and worship. In Romans 8:37 St. Paul says, 'In all these things we are more than conquerors through him who loves us.'

On the 23rd November 2020 Timothy Keller said in a podcast 'pray your tears'. There are prayers in the Bible which can help us cry out. Psalm 139:12 says 'Hear my prayer, oh Lord listen to my cry for help, be not deaf to my weeping.' The Lord Jesus knows pain, sorrow, isolation, and abandonment first-hand. He is a man of sorrows acquainted with grief (Isaiah 53:3). When we come to him in prayer and praise, we are like Job, who defiantly said, 'Though He slays me still I will trust him.' (Job 13:15). That is a rallying cry that has sustained me throughout the years that followed my Lake of Tears experience.

GLOSSARY

A TANNER
6p (old money)

GLYPING
Messing around

EEJIT
Eejit

CRAIC
Craic

LIKE LILTY
Rapidly

ALL REET COCK
How do you do

GI'E THESE BAIRNS
Give those youths

FGBMFI
Full Gospel Businessmen's Fellowship International

SIU
Spinal Injuries Unit

MICU
Manchester Interfaculty Christian Union

* Name changed to anonymise true story